Bee Stings...Bumble Bees

&

Butterflies

By: Stevie Flowers

www.beestingsandbutterflies.com

To: Marcia,
God Bless You!
Remember that
Faith always has a
future.

Love,
Stevie Flowers
11/19

Bee Stings…Bumble Bees & Butterflies

A Story of Survival

Copyright © 2016 – Stevie Flowers

RYF Publishing a division of RYF Holding Inc. LLC
840 Buckingham Cove Suite 200
Fairburn, GA 30213
678-744-3068
ISBN: 978-1544235707

Dedication

This book is dedicated to all of the women and men and their families whose lives have been adversely affected by the diagnosis of breast cancer and who had the tenacity to endure the many harsh realities of treatment and who now are the inspiration to others who are embarking on their journey towards survivorship.

This is also dedicated to the many nurses, physicians, specialist, nutritionist, surgeons, hair stylist, make-up artist, and other helpful souls who helped me step by step in my walk to complete healing and being Cancer Free.

My sincere gratitude is extended to my dear friend D. Lynn Roberts who was with me at every appointment; Sandra Mobley Terry for editorial guidance; Gaye Wilson for her editorial assistance; Dennis West, and A.J. for cover concept; and Mr. Steveland Morris for his continued support and encouragement to write and complete this book.

In addition, I dedicate this book to my incredible family; to my mother, Elizabeth deMontagnac, who served as my care giver through chemotherapy, radiation, surgery and nursed me back to perfect health with her unyielding love, kindness, constant care, and prayers; to my father, Cleveland Fike, Sr. who lost his wife of 40 years to breast cancer while I was going through chemotherapy. His strength never wavered in his support for me. He always was there with a joke and a smile for his baby girl; to my amazing daughter Nadera Nichelle Harris who I could always rely on to give me the best leg and foot massage when the pain and tingling seem to never end.

Finally, this book is dedicated to the memory of the millions of Queens & Kings of Courage who lost the battle, and who although determined to fight for their lives unfortunately didn't make it.

Table of Contents

Foreword

The very first time I met Ms. Stevie Flowers was at a banquet in my honor in 1981. I was standing in an elevator when I felt a soft kiss on the left side of my cheek. I heard a sensuous little voice say, "I'm sorry. I just couldn't help myself; I had to kiss you."

I said, "It's okay. What is your name?"

Again, the sensuous little voice said, "My name is Ruth, but my friends call me Stevie."

I said, "Oh, really? Using my name, are you?"

We both laughed and we have been great friends ever since.

Ms. Wonderful Flowers, as I call her, keeps a smile in her voice and shares the joy of her spirit with everyone she meets. No matter the circumstance or situation, I can always depend on her to make my day. She has always expressed kindness, love and care in the hundreds of voice mail messages she has left me over the past thirty years.

When Stevie told me that she had breast cancer, I was reminded of my first "Pure Love," Syreeta Wright and my "Perfect Angel," Minnie Riperton, who both passed away from breast cancer. Undeniably, they were both amazing Queens of Courage.

Stevie Flowers has proven herself to be an excellent author, which is no real surprise to me. I would not have anticipated anything less.

She often referred to this book as her "baby." Stevie has gone through labor and has delivered an exceptional life changing blueprint on how to fight cancer with the help of prayer, family, rest, alkaline water and possessing a positive attitude.

Bee Stings…Bumble Bees & Butterflies is a collection of stories that fill your heart with laughter, love, pain, joy and sorrow. It is a realistic adventure into the terrifying world of breast cancer and all that comes along with it. Her writing takes you from discovery, to exploration, to diagnosis, to research, to treatment, to surgery and finally to healing. I really enjoyed reading her book and I learned more about breast cancer than I ever knew before. I was blessed by it. I'm sure you will be, too.

Steveland Morris AKA Stevie Wonder

The Night We Met

December 7, 1981

Prologue

I have been a survivor since birth. Weighing just three pounds at birth in August 1959, God had a plan for my life from the start – to be a blessing to everyone whose life I have touched and whose life has touched mine.

In August 2010, I had my routine physical, Pap smear, blood test and mammogram. In September, my results came back with an abnormal Pap smear showing a probability that I could have contracted cervical cancer. Most cervical cancer is caused by a virus called human papillomavirus, or HPV. A person can get HPV by having sexual contact. You can have it for many, many years and not know it. There are many types of the HPV virus and not all types of HPV cause cervical cancer.

In addition to the abnormal Pap smear results, my mammogram came back showing calcification in my left breast that warranted further examination. Extremely concerned about the Pap smear, I started a regiment of tests to see if I had the HPV virus.

The first procedure was called a "LEEP", which is short for Loop Electrosurgical Excision Procedure. This procedure is used to diagnose abnormalities within the cervix. A very small portion of the cervix is cut and later is biopsied.

When the results came back negative, I was so happy…but I didn't go buy the White Star champagne quite yet. The next test was an "Endometriosis Canal" procedure, which was more painful than child birth!! OMG! I never felt so much pain in my life.

In between tests, I attended my family reunion in Maryland. I was staying at the house of my dear friend, Marvin. One day after my shower, I noticed a small boil under my left arm pit. Not thinking it was anything serious, I started putting warm compresses with baking soda on it, hoping to bring it to a head. After a few weeks had gone by, and many compresses had been applied, I discovered that the nodule was still there.

Finally, in December, my results for cervical cancer came back from my OB-GYN: NEGATIVE!!! All was well down on the south end of my body…Boy was I a happy girl.

On January 10, 2011, I called my primary physician, Dr. Andrews, and told her about the lump under my left armpit. She gave me a prescription for some antibiotics to take for seven days; all was well. Not! After the seven days, not only did the nodule not go away, but it was even more painful. Dr. Andrews suggested that I have an ultrasound performed on my armpit. Within two days, I was lying on a table at the hospital having an ultrasound done. I finished about 4:00 in the afternoon. Almost immediately, the radiologist who was looking at the results of my ultrasound asked me to give him my doctor's contact information. He then said her office would contact me the next day.

Sure enough, the next day I was scheduled for a biopsy of the lymph nodes in my left armpit. I was told to lie down on the table as I was given a needle in my armpit to numb the area. Then an 18-gauge needle was stuck down in my left armpit. I heard a snipping sound twice, and the procedure was over. It wasn't extremely painful, but it was uncomfortable enough for me to take the rest of the day off from work.

The next 20 days were filled with just a little bit of obvious anxiety. I was not worried, but there was a little bit of concern.

On February 1, 2011, Dr. Andrews called and said she needed to see me in her office the next day. My best friend, Lynn Roberts, went with me. When Dr. Andrews came into the examination room, her eyes were filled with tears. I asked her what was wrong and she said, "Stevie, you have Cancer." I think my initial reaction was that of disbelief, along with a little bit of, "What the blank, blank, blank did she just tell me?" It was like something in a movie; those four little words truly changed my life.

I then asked her, "Why are you crying?"

She said, "I'm so sorry that you are sick."

I said, "Don't be sorry. Please don't cry…I'm not crying. I need to know what needs to be done now and what my next move needs to be." Immediately, I felt confident and secure that this situation wasn't going to be the death of me. The thought **NEVER** entered my mind.

To be honest, I was more concerned about how my mother would take the news since I am the baby girl. I called her immediately from the examination room and told her what the test had revealed. My mother is a retired NICU (Newborn Intensive Care Unit) nurse, so she is not a stranger to hospitals, doctors or illness.

Mom said, "Let me speak to Dr. Andrews." She assured my mother that I was going to be fine and that we caught it in time. I knew that I was going to beat this thing, just like I cheated death out of a win as an infant. I knew that I was going to be fine, as always. NO WORRIES…

Introduction

"When FEAR comes knocking at your door… Simply answer it with unyielding faith!"
Stevie Flowers

When listening to medical professionals render a diagnosis of cancer – unless you have been told to go home and get your affairs in order – you must decide at that moment in your mind that, "I'm going to beat this thing." We can be healed by thinking positive thoughts at the very mention of the devastating possibility. Don't hesitate on claiming your healing!

If you start your journey with negative thoughts and energy in your mind and body, then you have already set yourself up for grand failure. Failure is not an option. Order up a cup of, "I'll Have Life" and go on with your day. It is truly that simple. Either you want to live or you want to die. Make the choice to live and this book will help you get through the rest.

Many of us are so very comfortable with the hope that doctors, medical professionals, pharmaceutical companies, and even the folks in huge government agencies really care about us.

Well, I'm here to tell you that they don't!! You are simply a number with a dollar sign attached to it. As far as they are concerned, you are only a revenue stream to be consumed by good old medical greed.

Cancer is an enormous money making industry that will get bigger and bigger as we become sicker and sicker. The truth is the drug companies and hospitals make money from sick people; not dead or healthy people, but sick people.

One day I was having a conversation with my friend, Ralph Johnson, who is the drummer for the world renowned group, Earth Wind and Fire. Ralph, who is a true believer in everything "Holistic", suggested that I do some research on a scientist named Royal Rife.

What if someone invented an electronic device that would destroy pathogens, bacteria and even viruses with no toxic side effects? What if that same device could wipe out cancer by altering the cancer's cellular environment or by killing cancer viruses with an electronic or ultra-sonic beam? Would you believe that it was accomplished years ago? The researcher who invented and perfected this device was Royal Raymond Rife. When you get some time, you should really do a little research on him.

The original Rife machine, based on a naval radio frequency oscillator, evolved to the Rife Ray Tube. It is the basis of Rife technology that underwent successful trials and experiments as it was developed in the 1930s.

You'd think that further research into Rife's findings would have been supported and encouraged further for the welfare of all; and at first it was. But guess what? Rife's technology was suppressed by the **Medical Mafia**. Very little has come of it in the United States. However, his machine is widely sold and used in Germany, Asia and other foreign countries. His story is only one of many who have made great strides in finding the cure for cancer, but was systematically dismantled because sick people are needed in the world to make the medical industry even wealthier.

Yes, sickness and disease are big money makers. There's got to be a better way to offer hope to the people. Well, after about a month of chemo, my sister, Gail, came to visit me to see how I was doing with my treatment. As usual, my dear friend, Lynn, was with me. We went to the treatment center to get my white blood cell shot. This is a necessary injection that will help to build my immune system, helping it fight off the negative reactions of the poison in my body. Without it, I may feel extremely tired, run down and totally out of it a few days after I have my chemo treatment. If your doctor doesn't offer it, ask for it. The way it is administered is that the injection goes into the fatty portion of your stomach. It burns a little bit, but after a chemo infusion, a single shot will not kill you.

It was such a beautiful day that we decided to go to a nearby park and enjoy it. We were talking and laughing so much I forgot that I had been in that chemo chair the day before. We called my sister, Debbie, and invited her to join us by Skype. As we were just sitting and enjoying each other's company, I noticed a group of bumble bees flying around gathering pollen. As I watched the bumble bees, I said to my sister, "Gail, I'm going to write a book and I'm going to name it **Bee Stings** (to signify the sting of cancer), **Bumble Bees** (which refers to gathering information regarding your treatment and general knowledge of your specific type of cancer), and finally, **Butterflies** (signifying one who evolves after a short time in a cocoon more beautiful and awesome than it was as a caterpillar).

It's a simple idea that has grown in my spirit; one that I know will bless many, many, many people."

The Bee Sting

The Bumble Bee

The Butterfly

The Bee Sting

In 1959 Richard Rogers wrote a beautiful song entitled: "My Favorite Things." It goes:

"When the dog bites, when the bee stings, when I'm feeling sad, I simply remember my favorite things and then I don't feel so bad."

Cancer stings you like you've never been stung in your life. But contrary to familiar bee sting remedies, it's not something that you can just put a Band-Aid on, rub an ice cube on, or make a tobacco paste to put on it and be cured. One thing that's for sure is that the sting doesn't go away immediately. Unfortunately, the treatments are a necessary evil. And, in cancer treatment, just like with the treating of a bee sting, you will feel really bad before you start to feel better.

The emotional impact of Breast Cancer can fill you with a number of crazy emotions. Shocked. Scared. Angry. Disappointed. Numb. Irate. Crushed. Brokenhearted. Furious. Overwhelmed.

None of us anticipates the sting of the "cancer bee." But when it catches you off guard, you have to stand up to it, face it and say, "I'm willing to do whatever it takes to alleviate the sting." You absolutely need to have a survivor's attitude and spirit. You must be committed to running the course. It will take plenty of hard work and a few tearful moments. It might even take your life. Just be prepared to put up a Muhammad Ali fight. "Float like a Butterfly and sting like a Bee". When it's all said and done, you'll be sitting on a tropical island in Dubai, sipping tea with the honey you've squeezed from that cancer bee. The sting will finally be gone…you will be cancer free!

The Bumble Bee

Have you ever had the opportunity to watch people's responses when a bumble bee comes around, especially children? When they see a bumble bee, they get both excited and afraid. They move out of the way, swatting and swinging, doing everything in their power to get away from that big black and yellow bumble bee.

Bumble bees are considered to be beneficial insects because they pollinate crops and plants. For this reason, I chose the analogy of the bumble bee because they gather vital information and spread it from place to place. In essence, it's the bumble bee's responsibility to bring forth life through pollination.

As breast cancer patients, we are like the bumble bee because we are searching for ways to maintain life. We are urgently gathering information, reading numerous books and surfing the World Wide Web. We do all of this buzzing around in hopes of gaining clarity on what our medical professional has told us, and what could possibly be in store for us in the cancer treatment arena. We may strike up a conversation with someone we know who has walked a few miles in our shoes. We find ourselves searching for clues on how our cancer may respond to treatment, constantly looking for as much information about support groups, resource agencies, clinical trials, etc. We are searching for help with insurance benefits, looking for help to get coverage for certain tests and treatment.

Well, to these bumble bees, I say, "Look no further!" This book is my way of helping you gain as much information at one time, in one place as you possibly can. This is the benefit of the bumble bee theory. Don't be afraid of what you may discover.

Remember: knowledge is power.

The Butterfly

That butterfly really means business when it's trying to get out of that cocoon. It's not an easy thing to do; it has to push and fight to get out. And as it pushes, it uses every ounce of strength trying to extend its beautiful wings and stretch its little legs to finally make its way out of that cocoon.

The transformation of the caterpillar inside the cocoon is nothing short of a miracle. It's amazing to know that something so unattractive will morph into a breathtakingly beautiful butterfly.

Life calls for strength. We need insight. We need courage. We need greater awareness, and often, we want to attain those easily. We don't want to struggle. We gain strength by facing up to what must be confronted. We grow through experiencing and overcoming. That's what I call the foundation of a true survivor.

The only way we can unfold and expand is through developing our mental, physical and emotional strengths. The reality of breast cancer will make you bring your "A game" of determination. It will make you utilize many of the talents and abilities that you never even thought you had. It will also make you stick to the course of having a positive outcome while, at the same time discovering what you are truly made of.

If I waved a magic wand and made everything alright, would I really be any better off? I would have gained nothing from my experience. As you work through the various stages of treatment, you must be certain to keep your eye on the prize.

Like my granny, Mrs. Annie Belle Pennick, would tell me, "If it doesn't kill you, it will make you stronger."

The butterfly, when it gains strength to fly, is not going to squeeze itself back into that cocoon again. Neither should you. So don't look back; keep moving forward, looking straight ahead. The butterfly stage of cancer is when you realize that you have evolved. You've gone through all the things you never thought you'd make it through.

You have dealt with the bee sting of cancer. You have overcome chemotherapy treatments, radiation treatments and possibly mastectomy or lumpectomy. So now, at this point, it's time to become a butterfly. It's time to evolve with all of your treatment being over, all of your research being done. Now you can walk proudly with your new hair, your new breast, your new attitude and extreme confidence. You are now ready to take on the world with your new testimony and renewed faith. Excited about being a walking miracle, you can stand strong, willing to be the inspiration for someone who is newly diagnosed and may need a helping hand.

This reminds me of my sweet friend, Media, who waited five years to come out her cocoon to get her reconstructive surgery. Her husband, Ricky, loves on her in a way he never has before. He is so proud and pleased with his new Butterfly Wife; he could not believe what a difference a little surgery would do to make her feel complete.

She is experiencing a newfound confidence that helps her understand what she is truly made of. Get out there and spread your wings, you butterfly!

Part I – Bee Stings

It's Okay

On a Monday morning shortly after my initial diagnosis, I had a 6:00AM appointment at Piedmont Fayetteville Hospital in Fayetteville, Georgia. At this point, I had already had a CT scan, a bone scan, mammogram, ultrasound, biopsy and numerous other blood tests. Going through so many tests and having so much blood being drawn from my arms, I was getting tired of being poked and prodded in search of that vital vein. I had never really gotten down about my initial diagnosis or had a pity party. I hadn't even shed a tear. I was just going through the motions of seeking out what type of cancer I had and doing all I could to keep a positive attitude and move toward the cure and treatment.

So I got up early to get to my appointment on time. When I got to the room, I began watching CNN on the television and filling out the paperwork. I was having a really good morning as always. Within less than 10 minutes, I was called back to the area where someone was taking my vitals. I was given a gown to put on and asked for a blanket because it was very cold back in the little hallway where I was sitting.

The attendant gave me a gown to put on and told me that Ms. Penny would come in to administer the dye into my arm so that they could see my organs on the MRI.

Within about 15 minutes, Ms. Penny came around the corner. As soon as I saw her with a needle in her hands and the vial of radiation that was inside a container, I immediately started to cry. I had not shed a tear until this point, but I guess the combination of seeing her coming towards me with the needle, and trying to be as strong and as positive as I could, I simply lost it.

A little old lady with red hair totally knocked me off my high horse of confidence. As tears rolled down my face, she said, "Oh baby, I'm so sorry. What's the matter?"

I told her, "It's nothing. It's not you. I'm okay, I'm okay."

At that moment, I was just so overwhelmed with so much of what I had been going through that I think the reality was just starting to settle in my spirit. And I knew that even though what she injected me with was for my benefit in the long run. I was still going to feel bad later that day because when that dye works its way through my body and, as it comes through the filtering systems of my kidneys, it really is quite uncomfortable. So I guess I was just at the end of my rope. I finally had a meltdown. As I wiped the tears away, I continued to tell Ms. Penny that it wasn't anything she had done, that I was okay. I understood that this test would help to determine what type of cancer I had.

Now, the fun part was going into the room getting ready for the MRI, which is something I had never experienced in my life. They laid me on a table inside of a tunnel kind of machine. Then she injected the black dye into my vein that would show up white on the MRI.

But to my surprise, I could not believe how loud the machine was, lots of *Noise, Noise, Noise!!!* It's amazing how engineers can make a machine that is so good at taking pictures of the inside of your body, but for whatever reason, they can't make it quiet. It bangs and bangs, so loudly, that I was given headphones to listen to music. Well, I asked her what type of music she had. She told me she had some country music, some blues and Marvin Gaye. Well Marvin made my day, I laid there with the headphones on for about 20 to 35 minutes. I still heard the banging through the headphones, but I was comforted knowing that at least we might be able to pinpoint where my cancer was really coming from.

The outcome of the test showed that there was cancer in my throat, my pectoral muscle, and some of the lymph nodes in my arm pit. In addition, I later found out on a molecular level I had, 57% cancer in my breast, 19% in my lung, and 12% in my skin. I was really sick, and didn't even know it. I was feeling just fine. But at half my best I'm still better than most. Praise God!

It Hurts

Coming out of surgery after having a lymph node biopsy, and my chemotherapy port installed, I found myself in a great deal of pain and discomfort. I had no idea I had been in surgery for almost three hours. As I was waking up in recovery, I saw my dear friend, Lynn, sitting there looking at me. With tears running down my cheek, I said to her, "*It hurts.*"

She told me later that she really wanted to laugh at me because I looked so pitiful, but couldn't. She felt so sorry for me.

Both sides of my upper chest were feeling like I had been hit by a truck. I was so sick and hurting. Even worse, I was upset because, in less than 20 minutes, I was being kicked out of the hospital. I told the nurse, "I don't feel so good."

She said, "You'll feel better when you get home."

What??? I could not believe that the nice people who checked me into the surgery clinic kicked my sick butt out on the curb without a second thought. Insurance companies have to determine what works best for their bottom line, not necessarily what is best for the patient. They will put you out of the hospital in a relatively short amount of time. And it really doesn't matter if they believe you're ready to be released or not. In other words, "You don't have to go home, but you gotta get the Hell up out of here."

Guard Your Space

Throughout my entire journey, I have been given a great deal of advice and wonderful words of wisdom. However, three of the most profound words I've ever been told were, "Guard your space!!!!" These words were uttered to me by an extremely exquisite woman who I call Mrs. C.

I met Mrs. C when I joined The Olivet Church in Fayetteville, Georgia. She was the first person at church I told that I had cancer. One Sunday morning, I was at my greeter's station doing what I do best (making people feel welcome when they enter into my church). Mrs. C came out of the sanctuary. I motioned her to come to my end of the hallway. We met in the middle; she immediately gave me the warmth of her smile and a comforting I love you hug. I whispered in her ear, "I have breast cancer."

With softness in her voice and love in her heart, she said, "Guard Your Space, Stevie. You are going to be just fine. Just stay faithful." That's exactly what I have done. Sometimes I don't feel like allowing some people into my space, it's okay to be selfish, especially when you're working at saving your life.

But likewise, you need positive, supportive, people in you space.

Faith Always Has a Future

Perhaps like most people with cancer, I was attempting to absorb all the information that was rapidly coming at me. In my case, there was very little time to do extended amounts of research. There is an inherent tendency for cancer patients to put our faith and trust in our oncologist, pharmacist, surgeons and others to make us feel better and secure. But I believe in a mighty God; one who can heal the sick, make the blind see and raise the dead. Still today, He is performing miracles for those who trust and believe in His Word. My God is the same God who was with Moses in the desert, got Jonah out of the belly of the whale, fed the multitudes with two fish and five loaves of bread and made wine for a wedding party that lasted seven days.

My cancer was the size of a mustard seed, compared to the parting of the Red Sea. God made sure I was in the company of likeminded and like spirited people who, like me, believe that prayer changes things. I had hundreds of people praying for my healing. From the little old ladies in the homemaker's club, and exercise buddies at my community center who all put my name in the prayer box at all of their churches, to the members and friends at my mother's church home in San Antonio, Texas to my sister, Debbie, who would put her prayers for my healing in her Sunday morning solos at her church in Baltimore, Maryland. My mother, Mary Wyse, requested that the members of her church in Pasadena, California, and my former church, West Angeles Church of God In Christ in Los Angeles, California, have me in their prayers. Finally, my new church

28

home in Fayetteville, Georgia, also known as "The Thrill on the Hill, where families fellowship in Fayetteville". The Olivet Church, kept me lifted in prayer. There is no limit to the power of the saints who are all praying as a unit for the same purpose. They were all praying on one accord for my steadfast faith and complete healing. Faith always has a future, and I am 100% certain that future is to be the foundation of a testimony.

Is That the Real Stevie Wonder?

My daughter, Nadera's 16th birthday was January 6, 2011. During this time, I was going through various tests and biopsies to determine what type of cancer I had and where it had originated from. I was so involved with my situation that, for the first time in her life, I was unable to give her a birthday celebration.

As time progressed, the test determined that I had stage IV breast cancer. Aggressive chemotherapy was needed immediately in order to stop it from spreading to my lymphatic system. From the day I was diagnosed, my dear friend, Stevie Wonder, was there for me. I told him that I wanted to have a party for my daughter, Nadera (his God daughter). He said, "How can I help? What do you need?"

On Friday, May 8, 2011 at the Castleberry Lofts, an intimate event venue in Atlanta, Nadera celebrated her sweet 16th birthday in grand style. With 40 of her classmates; close family members like her Uncle Marvin from Maryland; Grandma Ann from San Antonio, Texas; her stand in dad, Reginald; and other special friends and guests – it was a stellar event.

As her guests had been partying for quite some time, Steve called on my cell and said, "I'm outside," Oh, my God! I could not believe it…he actually was here, a true man of his word.

I walked outside and there he was, accompanied by his beautiful daughter (whose 16th birthday party Nadera attended when she was 5-years old in Santa Monica, California) and Steve's handsome son…Wow! I was so happy and elated to see them both.

As I escorted Steve into the party, all I could hear from her young guests was, *"Is that the real Stevie Wonder?"* He walked in and hugged Nadera, who was totally surprised. She had no idea he would be at her party. He sat at a table far in the back, ate a special meal I had asked the chef to prepare for him…sautéed spinach and baby Bella mushrooms in garlic & olive oil.

Nadera's guests were really amazed when he went to the stage. This is where they could see that it really was him. He took the microphone and started singing "My Nadera Amore." Immediately, cell phone cameras were snapping photos, and the song was instantly YouTubed. He then started to sing his version of "Happy Birthday" to her as we passed out her cupcakes. It was a moment of pure magic, as only God could have orchestrated.

Steve stayed almost three hours with us, and took pictures with everyone. Even my photographer friend, Tim, got a picture with Steve. It was a totally rare and special moment for all who attended. Steve showed off his dancing skills by dancing the "Cupid Shuffle" with me and our mutual friend, Tezona. The evening was truly an "I Wish" moment that came true. All I could say was, that is the real Stevie Wonder who brought incredible" Joy inside My Tears."

Steve, Stevie & Nadera

Oh, I'm Late for Chemotherapy

With the exception of the very first time I went to chemotherapy, I made sure I was late for chemotherapy treatment every time after that. It wasn't that I was extremely late; maybe about 15 to 20 minutes. I made sure when I showed up that I was looking good and smelling great. I would have all of the nurses and other patients thinking that every week I had just gotten off of a cruise ship or maybe I had just flown in from Dubai or Monte Carlo.

I would have this fantasy trip that I had come from. I would tell them I was late because my entourage was held up coming through customs. I would be smiling and laughing like I had just gotten off of Magic Johnson's private jet. I always came to chemotherapy with a family member or close friend; I was never alone, ever.

I was blessed not to ever have to drive myself to or from chemotherapy treatment. I'm just blessed that way, but others are not as fortunate. There are other people who have to take themselves to chemo by train, subway or bus. If you are in that predicament, don't be afraid to ask for help. Use the resources that are available. Someone will be more than happy to take you or pick you up from treatment. You simply just have to ask.

Your chemotherapy experience can be whatever you want it to be. Having a vivid imagination can truly come in handy for you. It's just like the serenity prayer, *"God grant me the serenity to accept the things I cannot change, courage to change the things I can, and wisdom to know the difference."* Most things in life are what you make of them. Chemotherapy is no different than any other circumstance. It's not what you do, but how you do it!

Smile even when your heart is hurting...

Off with My Hair

Two weeks after my first chemotherapy treatment, I noticed that the hair on my head was really getting thin. I could literally pull my hair out with my fingers. My eyebrows and eyelashes slowly faded in as many days.

My sister Debbie, who I affectionately call Sister Johnson because when she gave her life to Jesus Christ, she really became a REALLY new creature in the Lord. Hallelujah!

When Sister Johnson's husband of 25 years, Van, found out I was diagnosed with breast cancer, he told his wife that she needed to come be with me then, and very often.

During this particular visit, Sister Johnson flew in from Baltimore on a Wednesday evening, right in the middle of a chemo week. The next day, she woke me up asking me if I needed anything. I told her no. She then took her hand and brushed the side of my face, touching my sideburn. My sideburn came off in her hand. Later that day as we were just sitting and talking, she said, "Sissy, you are going to be alright." She then touched the other side of my face and the other sideburn came off, too. I always had more hair than she did, so I kind think she ripped them off on purpose. (Lol)

I decided not to wait for the hair to fall out. The very next morning, we got up early, drove to my friend Jamie's barber shop and he shaved all my hair off. Another way I took control of my situation…I was Bold, Bald, and Beautiful.

I Want What She's Having

On the right side of the chemo lounge in the corner is where I would sit with my back against the wall so I could get a look at everyone who came into the room. The patients that may have been a lot sicker than I was were seemingly on the other side of the room. On my side of the room, there was a strong feeling of life. There was laughter! There was music! There was talking and yelling. We were having fun and I made sure of it.

Many of the people who were on the other side of the room would always ask the nurses, *"Can I have what she's having?"* I refused to let my time in the chemotherapy lounge be filled with sadness. I would make it a point to greet everyone in the lounge, always with a smile and a positive attitude. Knowing that an act of kindness can be contagious!

I felt that this was the last place on earth that I needed to be negative, so I made lots of friends and acquaintances. I would bring food for people. In fact, we would have a potluck day some days. The bottom line is when you're going to that chemo lounge; you need to think of it as a positive because there are enough ugly toxins going through your veins in the form of chemotherapy. I encourage you to smile and be happy; truly believing that it'll be over soon.

Happy Hour: Tequila Style

I have one of the sweetest and finest uncles anyone could ever have. His name is Luther Douglas Pennick. He's my mother's baby brother; we fondly call him Uncle Hunka, or Hunka for short. Uncle Doug and I are only 10 years apart. We were raised more like brother and sister, rather than niece and uncle. We lived in the same house for many years. One of my very

34

first memories of my uncle Doug was on a Sunday when I was 5-years old. He was riding his friend, Jake Forsyth's brand new 3-speed English racer bike up and down the street. I asked Uncle Doug, "Please take me for a ride with you."

Uncle Doug picked me up, put me on the side of the sissy bar and said, "Keep your feet out." I said okay.

Before he could even get off the sidewalk, my right foot was in the spoke of the front wheel of the bicycle. Did I scream and holler? Yes! My leg was killing me. Hearing my screams, my grandfather came out of the house with a pair of pliers and a screwdriver and started taking apart Jake's brand new bike. Uncle didn't have a good day that day. I don't remember Jake being pleased either.

Likewise, he would keep all the men away that I didn't want to be bothered with. We always had a good time. My uncle Douglas has walked me down the aisle twice. If I asked him to give me away again, he would probably throw me this time. Lol.

I can remember so many wonderful times when my uncle would come visit me while I was living on the west coast. Uncle Doug came out to Los Angeles when I was a part of the event planning team for the NAACP Image awards. I picked him up from the airport in a stretch limo with a beautiful lady friend of mine. The rest of the story, he would have to tell you…I didn't get to see him much the rest of the weekend. He was walking the red carpet and conducting himself strictly like a VIP every time I saw him. Lol! As my dad would say, Uncle Doug was walking in high cotton; that's for sure!

Hunka came to San Diego, California when I secured the

contract for five Super Bowl parties. I was the floral designer for the owner's tent, the post party and three other events. He rode with me from San Diego to Los Angeles, where I had to pick up vases. I had custom made centerpieces that looked like mini Heisman trophies.

By the time Sunday came and the pre-game was on, Uncle Hunka wasn't moving. So, with my crew, I jumped into a truck, loaded up 200 centerpieces and made it happen. By the time we got to the San Diego Marriott, the room was already set with huge Jumbo Tron TV's all over the walls. I called my uncle on the phone, who was at my house watching the game. I said, "Hey, Uncle. You really should have come with me to help set this thing up. How many big screens do you need to watch the Super Bowl game?" I still tease him today about the game that he didn't get to see the way I got to see it…The Really Big Show!!!

When my dear uncle Hunka was told by my mom that I had breast cancer, he was genuinely upset. I then called him the next day. We spoke for a little while; he was so upset that he had to get off the phone. About two days later, he called me and said, "I'm coming to see you." I was so happy that he was going to fly from Baltimore, Maryland to Atlanta, Georgia to see me! The week that he came was a non-chemo week…yeah!! I picked him up from the airport and we came back to my home. I had gotten some great news that only a small area of cancer was still in my left breast. My body was responding greatly to the chemotherapy.

We had lot to celebrate, I decided as we were talking on the phone to my brother in Texas. I said, "Let's drink a toast to the way my body is responding. I've got a cigar we can celebrate with." My uncle had never smoked a cigar in his life. We were outside on my front porch and I told my uncle not to inhale cigar smoke. "Simply take a puff and blow the smoke out," I told him. It didn't go over too well because he ended up inhaling the cigar smoke and got really, really fuzzy in the head.

We sat on the porch well into the night. Both of us were feeling so very grateful that we had this time together, realizing that we were creating more magical moments. We had so many memories to talk about in how God was saving my life. We were just so grateful for His grace and mercy and most of all for our generation of favor.

The following Monday, I had to go back to my doctor and chemotherapy. Uncle Hunka went with me. Of course, all the nurses at the cancer center were commenting on how handsome my uncle was. A Teddy Pendergrass look alike, he is 6' 2", 230 pounds…very easy on the eyes. Uncle Doug and I were in an examination room with my oncologist; He was typing some information on my medical chart and telling my uncle how pleased he was with the way my body was responding to the chemo. My uncle proceeded to tell my oncologist that we were drinking shots of tequila on Friday night. My doctor didn't seem to have a problem with that at all; he just kept typing. Then my uncle said to my doctor, "Um, she was smoking cigars."

My doctor stopped typing and looked at me and said, "What are you doing smoking cigars?" I told him they were expensive and that I knew how to smoke them. It was the funniest thing. I told my uncle I would never take him to the doctor with me again. It turned out the tequila and cigars didn't interfere with the success of my treatment. However, I didn't dare do that again!!!

The point of this story is my uncle truly loves me and always wants the best for me. His intentions in telling my doctor were good. He wanted to make sure that my doctor knew what I was doing in case it would inhibit my healing. Sometimes when you're going through, you might need to take a swig of something to just calm down. Don't overdo anything; things in moderation will not hurt you. But if your doctor tells you not to, don't do it. We are all individuals and what works for someone else might not work for you. The most important thing in going through your survival is doing what you need to do to make yourself feel better.

Hawks Game

The week before I started chemo, a few of my friends traveled to Atlanta for my daughter Nadera's birthday celebration. One of those people is my oldest friend, Marvin. Knowing he is an avid basketball fan, I called my friend Carol (who works for the Atlanta Hawks) and asked her if she had four tickets to an upcoming game. Unaware that I was going through cancer treatment, she called me back as I was getting my first treatment. I told her what was going on and she was stunned to hear the news, like many of my friends. I assured her that I was just fine. Remember, attitude is everything.

Carol told me that she had four tickets for that night's game. I thanked her and asked if she could put the tickets in my friend's name, just in case I wasn't feeling up to it. I was picked up from chemotherapy, went home, rested a little bit and got in the car went down to Phillips Arena to watch the game. Because chemo can suppress your immune system immediately, my

38

oncologist advised me before I started chemo not to be around crowds of people. Well, that warning went right out the window. I made it a point that day to achieve a milestone. I wanted to raise the bar in my ability to still function as close to normal as I possibly could.

So, there I was watching the Atlanta Hawks game in the company of three of my dearest friends. About five minutes into the fourth quarter, I started feeling extremely tired. I looked at everyone (who were all keeping a close eye on me) and said, "It's time to go!" and we laughed. As we were leaving the aroma of French fries floated pass my nose. I said, "I want some French fries." It felt good to have an appetite; I had not been hungry all day. We left the building; I came home, got in my bed, and rested very well. What a way to start treatment: living, loving, laughing and making memories.

Family Reunion 2011

"It's so nice to see all the folks you love together, sitting and talking about all the things that's been going down..."

This is part of the lyrics of a familiar song recorded by the R&B trio, "The O Jays." There is no better way to describe what a family reunion is and should be. Every year on my father's side of the family, we have an annual family reunion that travels from state to state.

In July of 2010, we took a vote as a family as to where we were going to have the following year's family reunion. We decided on bringing the 2011 Fike/Haley reunion to Atlanta, Georgia, and that I would be the host. I started planning activities, making hotel reservations, securing the venue and caterer in

39

January 2011. After all, as an entrepreneur, event planning is what I love to do.

You might think that, after discovering that I had breast cancer the following month, it would have made me come to a screeching halt with my planning.

Not!!!! Once the family found out that I had been diagnosed, my Aunt Fleta, who is the matriarch of my family, and my sister, Debbie (Sister Johnson), suggested that it might not be a good time for me to host and organize the reunion.

Initially, I had a little attitude about their concerns. I assured them that I would be perfectly fine, and that I needed to be with my family now more than ever.

I was very aware of my limitations; so I knew not to overdo it. I also listened to my body, made sure I was drinking plenty of alkaline water, and knew when to go someplace and sit down. As a result, about 30 of my family members attended the reunion. We visited The King Center and Museum, and thanks to my sweet friend, Ms. Rosemary Jones, we enjoyed the media tour at the CNN building. The family feasted on an amazing buffet of fantastic foods, that was catered by my good friend, Ms. Bunny.

Everyone really had a wonderful time. They were so impressed at how well organized all the events were.

It wasn't until later that evening, after a full day of being the "hostess with the most" that I began to feel a little bit fatigued. My big sister, Gail, was trying to get me to dance with her. And I did keep pushing myself further, and believing that "at half my best, I'm still better than most." Not this night, though.

I tried, but at this point in my journey, I had already endured 18 weeks of chemotherapy, and I just didn't have the energy. (See, I'm not Superwoman.)

The next day, we all went to Sunday morning service at The Olivet Church. My Pastor Howard Creecy, Jr., had planned to meet us at church. He called me when we were on our way to church to apologize for not being able to meet the family. Unfortunately, he was in Washington, D.C. helping his daughter move into her apartment.

Tragically, two weeks later, my friend and pastor suddenly passed away. I will always cherish that last conversation we had when he apologized to me for not being able to meet my family. More importantly, I was able to show my family how much they all mean to me, and how grateful I am to have all of them.

Don't wait until a loved one becomes ill or in hospice to show them how much you really love and appreciate them. I encourage you to tell someone you love them each and every day. Please don't delay because you might not see them another day.

Attitude Is Everything

When I embarked on my first outside sales position, my manager gave me a book entitled *The Power of Positive Thinking* by Norman Vincent Peale. The principles I learned from that book have carried me though my entire life. Those principles are quite easy to understand and to put into place in your daily life. My whole life, I have always maintained an extremely positive attitude. God knew to surround me with family members who all felt the same way, so I had no choice but to succeed in every opportunity that I was given.

Life is full of ups and downs. There are good times and bad times, but I'm grateful that I've learned to trust in God. I'm grateful that I can place every care upon Him and really believe that He will work things out for my good. I know that's a lot easier said than done, particularly when you have been given what many would determine to be a death sentence. But again, attitude really is everything. Making sure you maintain a positive attitude about every aspect of your life will allow you to grow and maneuver in ways that are the prelude to miracles. At the end of the day, remember that life is just a moment, so enjoy it!

Making the Best of a Messed Up Situation

I went to see, my breast specialist. He finally came in to see me after I had been there an hour and a half. He started the ultrasound; he looked at my left breast, trying to find the infected nodule. He could not find it, so I had another mammogram. He still could not find it. He was trying to be as sincere as he could in telling me that the only way to be sure we had arrested all the cancer in my breast would be to remove it completely.

I had already had this discussion with my oncologist just days before. So, I decided to have both my breasts removed!!! Wow…All day I had been pretty alright with it. I was making jokes about having reconstructive surgery to make my breasts 32 double Ds. Lol! As usual, Lynn was with me; always by my side through thick and thin!!! The reality of surgery was setting in, but having faith that I would be completely healed never wavered because God said it, I believe it and I'm taking Him for His Word.

Everyday life still goes on, even after you accept the fact that you are facing a life- threatening, life-altering event. I put out the trash, put the groceries away, shed a tear or two and called my brother, Junior.

I explained to him how frustrated and upset I was with the whole process I had been going through. For the first time, he told me that he had already been through what I was about to enter into. He had a brain tumor.

Subsequently, he had radiation therapy directed into his skull. He had never told anyone what he had been going through for the past few months. My brother explained to me that his doctors were keeping a close eye on his tumor. As God would have it, my brother's tumor responded well to the radiation and other medication. Today he is cancer free! HALLELUJAH! Praise God! Seeing him walk in his healing was great encouragement for me. I, too, am healed!

What the @? @?!&@?! Did You Say, Ed?

My oncologist suggested that I visit the radiation people to get an idea of what I could expect if I had to have radiation therapy. I went to the Piedmont Fayetteville Hospital for my consult. The doctor I was supposed to meet was not there, so I was given the honor of speaking to a dude named Edmond. Ed came into the room and said, "Based on my PET scan and your history, you will have to have at least 35 radiation treatments." (Note: A positron emission tomography (PET) scan is an imaging test that uses a radioactive substance called a tracer to look for disease in the body.)

43

What @? @?!&@?! did you say, Ed?" He basically said that I had to definitely have radiation and that I would have to wait a year for any breast reconstruction. Like a rapid fire sub machine gun, he came at me with another round of bullets and said, "You need to make a decision as soon as possible."

I said, "Whoa! I know my doctor didn't send me here for you to tell me this!"

Ed said, "I don't know what your doctor sent you here for me to tell you. All I know is based on your history and your clavicle wall..." Again, I said to myself, "What the @? @?!&@?! is he talking about?" Talk about busting your bubble and not being prepared for such news! He brought tears to my eyes. The good thing about that experience was the shock he brought to my system made me come home that day and start writing my book.

Second Opinion

We have all heard that a lot of doctors seem to have a God-complex. They feel that way because we put them on pedestals and help them to believe that they are gods. Like a magic wand, we bestow all our faith, our love, our hope and all of our dreams into believing that they are going to heal us. And that's okay because we want to get better. We want to feel better; and, most of all, we want to live.

We want to put our trust and faith in our doctors, surgeons, oncologists, radiologists and all of those specialists that they send us to in order to see what's wrong with us in the hopes that they can help us.

My very first impression of my medical oncologist was a

negative one because I had been told on a Tuesday that I had cancer and the next available appointment he had was the next day on a Wednesday at 8:30 am. A good friend, Reverend Gary, from my church drove me to the appointment. My internist office, had been given an incorrect address. Gary and I were looking for a specific building and when we got to the building, the cancer center was no longer there. What the heck? This was about 8:00 in the morning, and I wasn't happy!

My heart of hearts was saying, "I'm not feeling this". I'm angry because I've just been told I have cancer. I came all the way down here to this building and there was no one there.

The cancer center has moved and nobody in the previous building knows where they moved to. Talk about poor planning I was livid. I called Dr. Andrews' office and, of course, I gave the receptionist, Melanie, a couple words that she didn't deserve, but I was very upset. As Reverend Gary and I went back outside to get in the car, I saw the mailman and asked him where the cancer center was. Thankfully, he directed us to the very next intersection.

We got to the building, and as I walked up the stairs to the cancer center, I began thinking, "Why would you have a cancer center upstairs instead of downstairs?" But that's neither here nor there. We walked into the office and there were at least 10 people sitting there waiting to be seen. There was a note on the counter that said, "Having a staff meeting. Sign in and take a seat." What was going on here? Now, my blood was boiling. Not only was I sent to the wrong address, but he had the nerve to not be ready to receive me!

I was really upset so I called back to Dr. Andrews and I let her know, in no uncertain terms, how upset I was. I said, "Dr. Andrews, what kind of place are you sending me to? I am not getting a good vibe about this place. I've been sitting here in the lobby at least half an hour and no one has come out and said anything to anyone." I'm not sure what Dr. Andrews told the oncologist, but it must not have made an impact because when their meeting was over, instantly people started moving around the office. They were coming out of different doors and going into different rooms. The first name they called was Ms. Flowers.

I immediately had to start drinking that white chalk liquid and have a CT scan. When I met with my oncologist the first time, I told him how disenchanted I was with the whole situation. I also told him how they needed to do better about letting doctors know where they're located.

After having that conversation, we achieved a mutual respect and genuine affection for each other. It was not until I got to the end of my chemotherapy that I felt that my best interest was not being attended to. I had begun to feel like my oncologist was too busy to take care of me; I felt like he had too many patients. He had been sick himself with a heart condition and he was in no way prepared to take care of me and the hundreds of other patients that he had. I can only say, "Please don't ever compromise your health because of a relationship you have with your doctor."

It is a wonderful thing to have good feelings about your doctor, but when you start to feel that your care should be progressing in "Divine Order", and it isn't, it is time to get a second opinion or even a third opinion. You only have one life on this earth. You can always get another doctor. Not another you. Don't let anyone second guess your care. Aggressively seek a second opinion. Your life depends on it.

Mom, Dad I'm Home!

"What Satan tried to do for my harm, God made for my good."

I have said this numerous times throughout my cancer treatment. Although my cancer was an ordeal, I still maintain that it was truly a blessing. When I was 5-years old, my mom and my dad divorced. I remember the day that the divorce was final because I was there in court with them. I grew up in Baltimore, Maryland and I remember riding the bus to the courthouse with them because my dad didn't have a car. As I grew up, my mom and my dad always had a pretty good relationship. She was always very cordial to him because of us.

My mom is a very special woman. She understood how important it was for her to allow him to come see us. We went to see him during summer vacations, and he would come see us on holidays. Once he remarried, we were able to go visit him and my stepsister and brother quite often. However, growing up without a dad wasn't a lot of fun at all. In fact, I probably dated older men because I was looking for the affection and attention I rarely received from my father. I guess that's another topic for another book I'll write one day.

My father remarried a beautiful lady. Her name was Ernestine Mills Fike. About the same time that I was diagnosed with breast cancer, my stepmother was going through the same thing. She had been fighting it for over seven years. She was going through a lot of different treatments, including chemotherapy. For years, we never knew that she had been sick.

Ernestine was an amazing example of a Queen of Courage. She always had a gigantic smile on her face, and praised God for all he had done for her. An amazing woman of GOD. She was in the process of getting ready to have stem cell replacement to help cure her cancer. Unfortunately, she did not survive. Ernestine passed away in June 2011.

When I told my father that I had breast cancer, he was quite upset. When I told him about my surgery, he said, "Baby, I'm coming to take care of you and to make sure you are ok." The weekend before my surgery was also the weekend of the 100 Black Men Football Classic that is held in Atlanta. My dear friend, Beverly, always makes sure that I have a ticket to go. I had gone out that Saturday morning before the football game to run some errands. When I came home, my mom said, "I need to go to Wal-Mart. Can I take the car?" I said, "Sure. I'm not going to go out until later this afternoon anyway."

My mom left and I was just piddling around the house, getting my outfit together for that evening (somebody said 100 Black Men, I said I'm there!) and also thinking about the surgery I was going to have that coming Monday. Not long after my mom left, my doorbell rang. I said to myself, "Now who is this ringing my doorbell? A Jehovah's Witness or what?"

I got to the front door and I could see that there was a man standing there with what looked like bags of groceries. When I opened my front door and saw what I saw, you would have thought it was Christmas. That's how much joy was on my face when I opened the door and saw my father standing there smiling at me. My dad had driven from Durham, North Carolina that morning to be with me. I knew he was coming; I just had no idea when. He wanted to be with me before I went in for surgery so that I would be aware that he was there. But, more importantly, he wanted to fix me a good meal and have time that we could share some laughs and enjoy each other's company. I was so excited and so happy. So when my mother came back from the store, I said, "Mom, guess who's here?"

She said, "I know. He was here earlier. He left to go get some stuff to cook you some fried corn and bake you some chicken and all the other things like that your dad makes for you." By the way, my dad is a fantastic cook.

We sat down and ate breakfast together. I even recorded them on my iPod and took pictures of them; it was so funny listening to dad tell his war stories (Lol). Later on that afternoon, I got dressed to go out. Mom and dad were on their way out.

I left my house and went to the football game. I had a very nice time. I also went to an after-party that was pretty cool as well. Then, it was time to come home.

For the very first time in my life, at the age of 52, I was finally able to walk through my door and yell, "Mom, Dad, I'm home." I'm so grateful to God that I had the opportunity to have my mom and my dad in the same space, alive and kicking. I'm grateful that they were there with me to take me to the hospital and bring me home from the hospital together. I can only count it as simply amazing because that is something they were not able to do when I was first born.

What Ever Happened to Baby Jane

During my second week of chemotherapy, my mom decided to go to Wal-Mart, her favorite place. Anyway, before she left, she asked if I was hungry. I said no, that I had just had some apple sauce. Three hours later, she had not returned, I had taken a pill for nausea, which makes you sleepy. I woke up looking for my mom, but she had not returned. I waited another hour. Unable to go downstairs, I was forced to lie there and dream about food.

Finally, I had to call the food police...my best friend and life saver, Ms. Lynn Roberts. I called her and said, "I'm hungry." Within 10 minutes, she was there. When she came into my bedroom and looked at me, she said "I looked like my name should be Blanche (Joan Crawford in "What Happened to Baby Jane" when Betty Davis would not feed her.) I was looking pretty pitiful...(Lol!)

When mom did finally return, she was all smiles. She probably just needed a little time for herself. I'm so grateful to have her.

Fond Memory

Going through chemotherapy is something that can destroy relationships, marriages, friendships, courtships and families. Sometimes, chemotherapy patients isolate themselves from many of the people who they love and those that love them. Not knowing what to expect, you really are at your wit's end because you're scared; you're not sure of what your future will hold. Being a single woman and going through chemotherapy is more than a notion. Shortly before I was diagnosed, I met a very nice young man who was a fireman. We met at a cigar bar and after a few weeks we started dating.

Keep in mind that it had been quite a long time since I had been in a serious relationship. I decided to give it a try. I thought I wanted to be in a committed relationship, seeing and being with that special person often, calling each other three or four times a day. You know: the last voice you hear at night and the first voice you hear in the morning kind of thing.

When I had confirmation that I had breast cancer, I told him. His response was quite surprising to me. I explained to him that I wasn't sure what was going to be happening to me and that I didn't think it would be good that we continue the relationship.

He understood, but felt that, if anything **now** was when I needed him most, and that he would be there for me. So the relationship continued for a few most months.

Before I started chemo, everything was fine, emotionally, socially, intellectually, and intimately. Things were in a good rhythm. About four weeks into my chemo, I started feeling like the relationship was not working for me. I just didn't want him or anyone around. In the cancer arena, this is quite common. I didn't want to drag anyone, especially him, through what I was about to go through. With very little notice, I told him that it wasn't a good time for me to be trying to work at building a relationship. I thought it was best that we not see each other anymore. He was not very happy about it and, at first; he really didn't understand what was going on. But being an absolute gentleman, he accepted my wishes and backed off. However, he would still take me to my chemo treatments, pick up my prescriptions and we would have lunch on Tuesdays.

This special young man was still actively trying to be a part of my life. But I continued to slowly dismantle our relationship.

51

Chemotherapy put my body, mind, soul and spirit in the most distressing period of my life. It is a documented fact that many marriages don't survive breast cancer and its treatment. Chemotherapy can totally destroy your libido; it will make the PH balance of your vagina extremely negative.

Because I was going through so many emotions, I couldn't accept the idea that he sincerely wanted to love me and give me his undivided attention. All of the natural things that any normal person would like to have in a relationship, I simply had no interest in. My focus was solely on me and my ability to get through this thing. I was dealing with numerous emotions and constant thoughts of getting better.

One of the most powerful lessons I learned through this part of my journey was to tell someone entering into chemotherapy that has a husband, boyfriend, study honey, lover, etc. that before they start treatment, if at all possible, go on some kind of getaway with your mate. Be the woman that your mate fell in love with; making sure you make love to them in every way possible. Show your lover how important they are to your total wellbeing. Also show them how wonderful it is to have them as your partner. Spend a great amount of time showing them lots of affection and attention. Do all this because it could be a pretty significant amount of time before you might feel like doing that again. Just keep those fond memories in mind. Before long, you will feel like being back in the saddle again.

Part II—Bumble Bees

Water, Water!!

When my friend Yolanda found out that I had been diagnosed with breast cancer she immediately called me and said, "I am bringing you a bottle of alkaline water. I want you to drink this water every day for the rest of your life." At that time, I had no clue of what alkaline water was, and why it was so important that she wanted me to drink it.

Yolanda brought me the water and explained to me why it was so important for me to start drinking it before I started my chemotherapy.

The most significant reason is cancer cells cannot survive in an alkaline environment; they only grow in an acidic environment. Ionized (alkaline) water is a very good anti-oxidant, and is filled with electrolytes; that will help to slow down the spread of cancer cells, and ultimately will kill them. The alkaline water helped to dispose of all toxins in my body through my bladder. She also explained to me that the water filtering process (Kengen System) purifies water making it healthy alkaline drinking water, which is rich in minerals, purged of impurities, and free of contamination. I know you're thinking if it were that simple your doctor would have told you about it. Not So! Your doctor doesn't want you to know about it. In fact, when you search the internet looking for alkaline or ionize water systems there's a lot of negativity about it. Just keep in mind that cancer business' and cancer researchers are pharmaceutical company's gold mines. Yes, your oncologist and your radiologist all want you to get better but they want you to get better using their products.

My personal opinion is that many doctors are in the pockets of the pharmaceutical companies. No matter how good you think they are, they would rather prescribe you a pill to make you feel better than to have you get better in a holistic way.

Now understand that I was not a very good chemistry student, in fact my chemistry professor gave me a passing grade my senior year in high school so I could graduate with my class. But I understood quickly that, with all the minerals in alkaline water electrolytes are the most powerful. They are what cells use to maintain voltage and are the vehicle that carries impulses across your body to other cells. Your kidneys work to keep the electrolyte concentrations in your blood constant despite the many changes in your body every day. For example, when you exercise you lose electrolytes in your sweat. These electrolytes must be replenished to keep the electrolyte concentrations of your body fluids constant. So many sports drinks have sodium chloride of potassium chloride added to them (A.K.A. electrolytes). Another example is when small children have diarrhea, their stomach is upset, or they are vomiting your pediatrician tells you to give the child Pedialyte. What does Pedialyte contain? Electrolytes. The ingestion of the electrolytes helps the baby to regain much needed fluids, and retains the nutrients that they have lost with the diarrhea and vomiting. Again these electrolytes and fluids must be in place to prevent dehydration and seizures. The Pedialyte has sodium potassium in it just like sports drinks do, to hydrate the body, and build up the immune system. It's really not rocket science.

Yolanda invested in a Kangen water system, after she overheard someone talking about how it reduces muscle inflammation. At the time she was having problems with her knees, and constant back pain. Almost immediately her knees and back were feeling better, today she is pain free. Her nephew with diabetes started drinking the water and within 6 months his diabetes was gone. Yolanda's sister suffered with chronic arthritis, today her arthritis is gone. Now what really made me a believer was the story about her sister in-law, Harriett who was struggling with bone cancer in her back. Day by day she was slowly fading away. She weighed about 90lbs, when Yolanda first gave her the water three years ago…today she's cancer free, and has gained all her weight back. Now I don't expect you to go out and purchase a $4,000.00 water filtration system. However, check the internet for alkaline water machines. They are quite reasonable on E-bay. You can also go to any store grocery store or Wal-Mart and buy **Smart Water, or Eternal Water.**

By the time I started my chemotherapy treatments, I had probably a million electrolytes in my body from drinking the Kangen water. As a result of having all of the positive electrons and electrolytes in my body the alkaline environment made it more easily for me to get rid of the chemotherapy toxin that is left as residue in your body. Every day, every hour, I was drinking water. Therefore, on my chemo days my body was able to get rid of the overflow of the chemotherapy.

When you are getting your chemo therapy administered through your "drip", it is very important that you go to the bathroom often. I know it's going to be a little weird dragging your chemo IV stand with you to the restroom. But you can't disconnect at that time. Take my word for it you will be adding more years to your life, simply by getting rid of the excess toxins. Please Go Potty!! By doing that it releases all the toxins that are left over out of your bladder it and helps your kidneys to function properly. Drink the water...

As you know chemotherapy does attach itself to cancer cells that are infected. However, it can also stay in your body and affect your good cells. Chemotherapy can bring cancer to other parts of your body years later... So take my word for it you want to drink lots of smart water, or distilled water; drink a lot of water! I attribute a large portion of my success in beating my cancer was due to the fact that I drank electrolyte water all day every day; and still do.

Sitting in the Park

After about a month of chemotherapy my sister Gail came to visit me to see how I was doing with my treatment. As usual my dear friend, Lynn was with me. We went to the treatment center to get my white blood shot. A white blood shot will help to build your immune system to fight off the negative reactions of the poison in your body. Without it, you may feel extremely tired, run down, and totally out of it a few days after you have your CHEMO treatment. If your doctor doesn't offer it, ASK for it.

The nurse will inject the white blood cell shot into the fatty portion of your stomach. Burns a little bit, but after a chemotherapy infusion, a single shot will not kill you...lol.

It was such a beautiful day, that we decided to go to a nearby park and enjoy the amazing weather. We were talking and laughing so much I forgot that I had been in that CHEMO chair the day before. We called my sister Debbie and invited her to join us by Skype! As we were just sitting and enjoying each other's company, I noticed a group of Bumble bees flying around gathering pollen. It was at that moment I realized that I needed to tell people about my story. As I watched the Bumble Bees I said to my sister, "Gale I'm going to write a book, and I'm going to name it, Bee Stings, to signify the sting of Cancer, Bumble Bees, which refers to gathering information regarding your treatment, and general knowledge of your specific type of Cancer. Finally, the Butterfly evolves after a short time in a cocoon more beautiful and awesome than it was as a caterpillar. A simple idea which has grown in my spirit, that I pray will bless many, many, many people.

Can't Buy a Burp

There are so many fascinating things to discover about the anatomy of your body while you're going through cancer treatment. I had no idea what the sternum's function is. I, like most people, thought it was just that big bone in the middle of your body; the bone that holds all your other bones together, keeping your clavicle, vertebrae and your frame all intact.

I discovered that the sternum is one of the biggest producers of white blood cells in your entire body. The importance of white blood cells to a cancer patient is phenomenal. White blood cells help to build your immune system. The white blood cells circulate blood throughout your body. White blood cells help to fight off foreign invaders and infection in your body. On the Tuesdays after my chemotherapy, I would have to go back to the cancer center and get a white blood cells shot. They would take a needle and shoot the white blood cells in the fatty part of my stomach. It didn't really hurt it was just another pinch on my way to becoming a pin cushion. (By the time you get finished with cancer care, you are so very accustomed to getting

58

stuck all over the place with various needles. One more won't kill you.)

I have met some cancer patients who were not offered a white blood cells shot. It could have been for a number of reasons. I don't know, but should the need arise, please ask for it. With the white blood cells shot elevating the production of your white blood cells, your immune system will have a greater chance of not becoming compromised.

Since the sternum is very close to your throat, that means you may begin to have really bad indigestion. No matter what you eat, and no matter how little you eat, you are going to feel like you have the worst case of acid reflux ever recorded. This feeling of not being able to buy a burp is very frustrating.

Your oncologist has an array of pills that they can prescribe including Prilosec (the purple pill). Or, they may have you to take papaya, eat ginger or drink ginger ale. The only thing that helped me was peppermint. I would drink a little bit of peppermint tea or suck on a piece of peppermint candy. Either would help to promote the movement of those white blood cells that were conveniently assembled in my throat.

I wasn't angry with those white blood cells because they helped me to feel better, helped me to heal faster, and helped to give me energy to get up and get moving quicker than if I didn't have them reproducing excessively in my body.

So take my advice. It only lasts a couple days. But once it's done, you are going to really feel so much better, and your body will be stronger to fight the bee sting of cancer. Take it all with a smile, keep it moving and suck on some crystal blue peppermints. You'll get through it. I did!

Numb Toes, Black Feet and Fingernails

Most likely when you go for your very first chemo treatment you will be given what they call a chemo pack. Your chemo pack is a little package of drugs that you will need to help you with chemotherapy side effects. Your chemo pack should include Benadryl in case you have an allergic reaction and a small amount of Imodium in case you have diarrhea. You will also have some type of laxative: possibly Milk of Magnesia because you will, most likely, be constipated from the pain killers you will be taking. Also included in that pack will be an over-the-counter pain reliever like Tylenol.

As time goes on, you will be given other drugs that help you deal with other side effects from the chemotherapy. Make no mistake; there is a pill for any ailment that you have going through your cancer treatment. However, nobody told me nor did I read in any of my literature that my feet would be numb as a result of chemo. A year later, my toes are still numb and difficult to bend. If you are experiencing numbness in your toes, let your doctor know and they will prescribe something to take the pain away. Your oncologist might advise you not to get manicures and pedicures because you don't want to take the chance of getting a cut on your cuticle by a cuticle tool, which could lead to infection.

Don't fret. This is how to fix that: have your best friend or your husband, girlfriend, boyfriend, whoever gives you manicures and pedicures at home. Pull out that home spa pedicure machine that you have never used.

It really makes a difference. Your toes will be numb, but you'll have some pretty and soft feet because of it.

Within about two weeks of chemo treatment, I noticed that my palms started to turn black. I also noticed that my skin turned dry and began to peel. This, too, is a side effect of chemotherapy. Your fingernails and toenails will become visibly black. The area inside the nail will develop a large amount of black buildup, also stemming from the chemo. What happens is as the chemo circulates throughout your body, after a certain point it can't go any further. The tip of your nail is the last place for the chemo to go. It's like the leaves on a plant turning brown from being over watered. The same principle applies here. At that point, it starts to build up in the nail and will stay there until you stop chemo and your nails begin to grow out. It may take from six to eight weeks to completely grow out, but no worries; it will grow out.

It's not a pretty sight; but, again, nail polish can be your best friend. Just be careful using instruments and pushing back your cuticles. My feet were black and dry, and the palms of my hands were black and peeling. Also make sure you use some type of cocoa butter, like Palmer's, or a rich moisturizer, like Aveeno. Massage your hands and your feet often, from as little as two to as much as six times a day. If you follow these few little tips, it'll make it a lot easier to deal with your nails and your feet.

The numbness is going to feel really weird and it may never end. It's just something that you have to take with you. After a while, you will get used to it. When you see the black gone from your nails, you will really know that the chemo is finally out of your body. Thank you, Jesus!!

Oh, My Poor Aching Gums!

How many of us have minor dental issues? If you are ever diagnosed with cancer and you have to go to chemotherapy, I pray that your teeth are in good condition and that you have optimum dental care before your treatment begins. After a while, the chemotherapy is going to make your mouth feel like you need several root canals.

If you ever thought you had sensitive teeth, let me assure you that you haven't experienced tooth sensitivity yet. I suggest you start using Sensodyne toothpaste; spread it on your gums at night. Don't use anything with peroxide in it at all; just regular Sensodyne toothpaste. Not only will it be super sensitive, but you may develop mouth sores or blisters. Quite possibly, your teeth may fall out. Your oncologist can prescribe you something called Magic Mouthwash. My friend little Cindy Lu Hoo, (she really looks like Cindy Lu Hoo in the Grinch who stole Christmas) was having problems with her teeth and gums while going through chemo told me about the Magic Mouthwash. I quickly asked my doctor for it.

The most common recipe of Magic Mouthwash is equal parts of Benadryl, Maalox, Lidocaine and something called corticosteroid to reduce inflammation. I had no clue about this magic mouthwash until my gums became inflamed. You should swish it around in your mouth then spit it out using it three or four times a day.

My mouth was so sensitive I couldn't eat raisins let alone anything sweet. I didn't have a problem with cold sensitivity, but my mouth hurt all the time, especially if I tried to eat something sweet.

You will discover that the word cancer survivor is like a badge of honor. Cancer treatment is not for punks…forget that "sugar and spice and everything nice," stuff that girls are made of. Get tough...take out your earrings, spread on your Vaseline, and fight like a girl…Scratch, kick, and bite. Cancer will fight you back, and will bring its big sister, mother, brother and Big Mama to fight you, too.

Don't Ask, Don't Want

Trying to maintain your weight while going through chemotherapy and breast surgery can be very difficult. I have always had a slender build, but I've always had a great appetite. When I was diagnosed with breast cancer, I weighed 170 pounds. I was quite curvy and had plenty of hips & booty. Trying to maintain an appetite, while undergoing chemo was literally impossible for me. There were so many of my favorite foods that I wanted to eat so badly, but I just didn't have the appetite. I never had a problem keeping food down; I had plenty of nausea medicine for that.

My chemo day was on Monday, and I generally did well on that day. On Tuesday when I would go get my white blood cells shot, it seemed like I craved pizza. I would stop at a pizzeria to get a slice of spinach and feta cheese pizza. This worked for about three weeks after I started my chemo. After that, I could only dream about the food I wanted to eat.

My mother, who was my caregiver, would fix food as I requested. Every meal had either mashed potatoes and gravy or macaroni and cheese. One day, she decided to put some spinach on the side of my macaroni and cheese. I was so upset I told her, "If I don't ask for it, don't give it to me." All I wanted was what I asked for. If anybody put anything on my plate that I didn't ask for, it was totally unacceptable.

After that incident, my mom learned a very valuable fact: if I didn't ask for it, I didn't want it. As time went on, I still never wanted anything but mashed potatoes and gravy and macaroni and cheese. I stress the importance of this because your doctor is going to want you to eat. However, you're really not going to want to eat. But if there is one thing that you like, no matter how crazy it is eat it. It is better to have some type of nutrition in your body than nothing at all. You will want to eat some things that you used to like.

During chemo, you shouldn't eat from salad bars or any type of open buffet food. There is the possibility of infection from the publicly exposed food. You will have to be extremely careful about things like that. Once you get your food rhythm, you will be just fine. Just keep eating.

Rest Does a Body Good

If you are in a position to take six months to a year off from work when you're going through your cancer treatment, take it. You really are going to need that amount of time to rest and heal. After enduring pain in your treatment, pain in your recovery and pain from your surgery, it is of utmost importance to rest your body.

All of that trauma sometimes will have your body wondering, "What the heck is going on?" You want to create an optimum environment of healing which comes from resting. Maintaining an even balance of rest, eating, and an elevated water intake will help with the healing process. You can never rest too much when you're going through treatment. Just sit back and relax. Don't sweat anything. Most of all just lie down and be still. Your body will tell you when you've had enough rest; and your body will tell you when you need to go sit down. Just listen to it. Listen to that little inner voice.

Breast Cancer (BRCA) Test

African-American women are amazingly phenomenal in every aspect. As Maya Angelou says, we are, "So awesome that we not only have our sassy way of dance, dress, hair styles, and body stature." With our wide hips, big booties and baby soft skin, we are those who can take nothing and make something out of it.

Interestingly enough, we have our own style of breast cancer, too. It's called Triple-Negative. It is so intrusive to your body that it is extremely hard to treat. And, like some cancers, it is impossible to cure. A study found that African-American women are three times more likely than White or Hispanic women to be diagnosed with Triple-Negative breast cancer.

The differences in cancer characteristics weren't due to age or weight, both of which can affect hormone receptor and HER2 (one of the factors that make up Triple-negative) status. So, it's likely that genetic factors may be responsible for the higher incidence of Triple-Negative breast cancer in African-American women.

Other research has shown that, compared to women of other races, African- American women are:

- more likely to be diagnosed with breast cancer
- more likely to be diagnosed with advanced stage breast cancer, if diagnosed more likely to be diagnosed with

65

breast cancer that is aggressive and harder to treat
- more likely to have breast cancer come back
- more likely to die from breast cancer

As this study shows, it's likely that the greater risk of Triple-Negative breast cancer affecting African-American women partially explains why breast cancer in African-American women tends to be more advanced, more aggressive and harder to treat.

If you're an African-American woman, you can't change your genes, but you can make sure that any breast cancer is diagnosed at its earliest, most treatable stage. If you're older than 40 with an average risk of breast cancer, this means getting a mammogram each year. If you have higher-than-average risk, you may have a more aggressive screening plan that starts at a younger age. Between mammograms, make sure your doctor or other healthcare provider does regular breast exams. You also should consider doing regular breast self-exams. Tell your doctor right away if you find anything you're concerned about. If you need to know how to do a self-exam, ask your doctor.

See what I mean? We couldn't have a simple strain of breast cancer. Triple-Negative is like an extra gene or precursor that we are genetically born with. Very little research has been done on what I call "the anaconda" of breast cancer.

If you have a history of breast cancer in your family, please ask you medical oncologist to give you the BRCA test, commonly called the bracket test (and sometimes pronounced "bracka.")

OMG! This will be the easiest test to take in your entire life. Your doctor will give you a series of blood tests. They will give you a travel size bottle of Scope mouthwash. Swish the mouthwash around in your mouth, then (there is no nice way so say spit) spit the mouthwash back into the bottle, and ta-dah! You're done. They send the mouthwash to the lab. Two weeks later, you have your results. There's no good reason we are not getting tested. If you have a history of breast cancer in your family and you can't afford the test, contact The YWCA or The Susan G. Komen Foundation and ask for assistance. They are there to help.

I wasn't told about the BRCA test until after I had finished my chemo, and was seeking a second opinion. My original oncologist never even mentioned the possibility that I could save the lives of my daughter and sisters by having such a simple test. Prayerfully, I tested negative.

I Cried Because...

On Monday morning, September 26, 2011, I entered the hospital to have a bilateral mastectomy. In layman's terms, I was having the tissue in both of my breast removed. I had gone through my pre-op process weeks before and I was walking into the hospital with my mother, father and my best friend, Lynn. The only person that I was missing at that time was my dear friend and Pastor Howard Creecy Jr., who passed away July 28, 2011. There was a major void in my spirit because I knew that he would have been there with me.

Once I met my pre-op nurse, a beautiful lady named Shea, everything was okay. She was so amazing, so compassionate, sweet, kind, loving and caring. As she put needles in my arms that would later attach the IV to my body, she reassured me that I would be just fine. About that time, my dear friend, Ms. C,

Mother Jones and her husband, Deacon Jones from my church were standing at my bedside. We joined hands and they said a prayer for me right then and there. The sweet spirit of the Holy Ghost overwhelmed me and took control of my mind and my body. I lay there in confidence, knowing that my surgery would be successful and that I was going to have no fear because of it. As they rolled me into the operating room, I happened to see my surgeon, Dr. Rogsbert Phillips. I waved at her and said, "I know you." As always, I was in great spirits. I give total thanks to God, who is always in control.

The attendants put me on to this little table. I could not believe how small the operating table was. The attendant smiled at me and said, "Wow, you really fit on that table. There's no overflow." We laughed and made small talk. I was overwhelmed with the amount of surgical instruments that were all over the instrument table. I asked one of the attendants, "Are you going to use all of those?" She said, "Yup."

In disbelief, I said, "I don't have enough tissue on my body for all of those instruments."

They all laughed and then turned this huge light on. Wow, I could have gotten a pretty good sun tan from such a bulb (lol). But I can understand the fact that when the doctor is about to perform a surgical procedure, they really do need a 1000-watt bulb to see what they're doing.

As I made small talk with the attendant, I was telling them how excited I was going to be once I got my new set of breasts. My anesthesiologist walked over to me and said, "How are you feeling?"

I said, "I'm feeling fine!"

Then she said, "Well, in a minute, you're going to be getting the best sleep you've ever had." That's all I remember.

When I woke up, I could hear female voices talking loudly in the room. They were talking about what they were going to be doing that weekend and that they were going to have a party. I just thought it was so annoying. That's a very disturbing thing to wake up to. My dad had a look on his face that showed how disgusted he was. I gave him a look and he turned around and asked my attendant, "Could you please ask the ladies to be a little quieter?" I later discovered that my father was standing so close to me at that point because, I had motioned to him to come close to me. He told me that I whispered in his ear "I Love You Daddy". I have no recollection of that as I was coming out of the anesthesia, but he said that he had never felt such joy in his 80 years on earth.

In the meantime, I just wanted to sleep. It seemed like an eternity to get me to my room. I slept for a long time. When I woke up again, there was a nurse asking me if I was okay. I wasn't in any pain or discomfort. Yet, I felt so sick. The anesthesia was wearing off, which made me feel very nauseous; then, I felt the pain. The pain in my ribs on both sides felt like they were broken. Later, I discovered that a cadaver bone had been fused to the top part of my rib to build a ridge so my new breast implants would have support.

As I looked down, I realized that I had on a bra that had two pockets in it that were holding these "grenade looking bottles." These bottles were attached to me at my incisions on both sides of my breasts. They were surgical drains. Surgical drains help to prevent blood and lymphatic fluid buildup under your skin where lymph nodes have been removed, and promote healing

69

and recovery.

I was just a little bit drowsy and then, maybe about two hours later, a lady came into my room named Becca. She said, "Alright it's time for you to get up. I need you to go to the bathroom and I need you to let me take your catheter out."

Within less than 20 seconds, she had that catheter out. Becca had me up and going to the bathroom on my own. As I was walking down the hall, I could only take a few steps before I said, "Oh, my God! I'm going to be sick." I also said, "I can't do this right now. I need to go back and lay down." Becca asked me on a scale of 1 to 10 how much pain I was in. I was at least an eight, so she gave me a pain killer. I was so thirsty; I was glad my friend, Lynn, had bought some of my alkaline water to the hospital. I made the mistake of drinking too much water and immediately brought it back up. Later, I found out that it wasn't the water that made me sick, it was the anesthesia roaming through my body.

The next morning, I was awakened by my breast surgeon's assistant, who noticed that one of my drains was not draining properly and that I was in a great deal of pain around the top of my breast area. Dr. Diva as I call her, unhooked the bra to loosen the tube that was attached to the side of my breast. She actually moved it so that it would start the flow of the fluid. The good thing was the fluid and bacteria that were coming out of my body at that point started flowing. The bad thing was she actually shifted the expander that had been placed in my breast.

Expanders are a very hard plastic sack with a metal ring at the tip that allows saline solution to be injected into the breast. The expander is placed behind the pectoral muscle and is used to expand the muscle to the desired size that you want your breast to ultimately be. I woke up with as much breast as I had when I went to sleep. That's an awesome thing!

Although I was in pain, I still felt that something was wrong, so my cosmetic surgeon's assistant, whose name is Dr. Gary, came in and just unhooked my bra to see what my breasts looked like. Dr. Gary realized that the expander in my left breast had shifted and said, "Ms. Flowers, either I have to push it back into place or you're going to have to go back into surgery."

We all know I was not trying to go back into surgery, so I said, "Dr. Gary, do what you have to do," not realizing that my breasts were totally numb. He pushed and pushed and pushed to get it back into position. He put small magnets at the tip of the breasts to see exactly where to shoot the saline into the expander. The expanders create a space behind the pectoral muscle to let your body know that there's going to be something placed inside or behind the muscle. When my permanent implants are put in, my body will welcome them because the space has already been made for them.

I was given another pain killer and rested a while. When I woke up again, there was a lady bringing me some food. This lady was very nice. She smiled at me and asked me if I needed anything else. I could not eat the food that was given to me, so I just tried to drink the water and rest.

At 8:00, the day shift came in. The head nurse, Sam, and Becca were like night and day. Sam gave me the impression that she really wasn't having a good day. She really wasn't happy to be my nurse or anyone's nurse that day. They gave me more paperwork to read and told me that I would have to get up and walk, that I had to have a bowel movement, and that I had to eat something before I could leave.

As I was resting a young girl walked in with earphones on. She pushed my door open so hard that it hit the back of the wall. She then put a box of tissues in my room and walked out without closing my door. I was extremely annoyed by this, and asked her to come back and close my door. She kept on walking. Still in a great deal of pain, I pushed my call button on my bed and asked for a pain killer. Nurse Sam answered the phone and said "Okay, I'll be there soon". Two hours later, no one had come to give me a pain killer. So while I waited, I said to myself, "Well, I've gone to the bathroom and I have eaten a little bit. Let me get up and take this walk." I grabbed my IV and put my hand on the back of my gown to keep it closed and I started walking down the hallway. I walked from one end of the hallway to the other end of the hallway totally frustrated. While I was walking along, not one employee on that floor said hello to me or gave me any type of encouragement. I don't think I've ever felt so alone in my life. I felt like, "These people don't care anything about me. They act like they are numb to the fact that I don't feel well." When I got back to my room, I was upset and I just cried.

I then called Dr. Phillips and told her assistant exactly what was happening to me and how I felt like I was totally being ignored and neglected. I asked what had to be done so I could be discharged. I told her that I had already walked around, I didn't have a temperature, I had used the restroom, and I could sit up on my own.

Surely, it was time to go. And, most importantly, I was still in pain. The nurse never came to bring me my pain killer until I called Dr. Phillips and her assistant got in touch with a nurse.

I was so upset I called my mom and my dad. I said, "I want to come home. Please come get me." By that time, Dr. Phillips called me back and said she was going to have me immediately discharged. Would you believe that the nurse didn't arrive at my room with a pain killer until my parents were sitting there getting me ready to leave? When she offered me the pain killer, I said, "I don't want it now. I want to go home."

My mother said, "Take the pain killer. You will want it later." Thank God I didn't have to stay in the hospital and be treated like I didn't matter. I could go home and be with my mom, dad, daughter and my little dog who all love me so very much. An hour after my mom and dad got there, Dr. Phillips' office sent the paperwork and I was on my way home. I spent exactly 34 hours in the hospital.

I pray that no one ever has to experience the insensitivity I felt from the staff at this hospital. We deserve better care from those who call themselves care givers.

Is My Rib Broken?

When I woke up from my double mastectomy surgery, I was in very little discomfort. However, a few days later when I was lying in my bed (trying to get ahead of the pain) I felt like I had been hit by three freight trains. I also felt like an elephant was sitting on my chest and broke my ribs. If you've ever had the experience of childbirth, I know you thought that was something. Well, after facing what I faced, all I can say is, "Get ready for the Big Kahuna!"

We must be clear and understand that when you have a mastectomy, your breast surgeon is not removing your breast.

73

They remove breast tissue and a lot of fat. Once the breast surgeon is finished, he or she will step to the side and your cosmetic surgeon will step in. A cadaver bone is then fused to the top of your ribs to make a ridge above your ribcage to work as a brace that will later support your new breasts.

It feels like your ribs are broken as you lie there in extreme discomfort. As I said before, these drains are very important because they help control the flow of blood and lymphatic fluid that is draining from the surgical incision area. When you add being uncomfortable with those drainage balls to the fact that your ribs are killing you, you would wish you could have a stronger pain killer. But anything stronger would have probably put you in a coma. It hurt so bad for days and days and days and days. I thought that the pain would never go away.

It is so bad that it's something I can't even describe. I asked my doctor a month later why I was still in such pain. He said, "Unfortunately, fused bone take a long time to heal…it just does."

Oh, my God. The things that you don't know until after the fact. Eventually, the pain went away. There are still some days when there is discomfort; like when it's damp. It's almost like I can tell the weather by my rib cage. Sometimes, if I move the wrong way or pick up something a little heavy, I get an intense reminder of that cadaver bone. Stay mindful that, there's always a bright side inside of that dark cloud. There's always a rainbow after the storm. The price we sometimes have to pay first so we can have pleasure later. What's a little pain and discomfort when you'll never have to wear a bra again? You will be a woman with perky breasts when you are 80 years old. Now, that's a wonderful thing!

Decisions and Expectations

Many women who have a bilateral mastectomy are not fully aware of what exactly to expect with the surgery. Let me be the first to tell that you will not lose your breast. What you will experience is the removal of breast tissue. Unfortunately, this sometimes includes the removal of your nipple. I was a little upset at the thought of losing a perfectly good nipple, but joy does come with reconstruction. lol

I chose to have a double mastectomy for three reasons. The first was to limit the possibility of ever having breast cancer again. The second reason came from what I read in an insurance newsletter. It said that because so many women are being diagnosed with breast cancer in a single breast, if the cancer was to return in the other breast, the insurance company may refer to the return of the cancer as a pre-existing condition, and, therefore, deny treatment. The third reason was I took a long look at my right breast and said to myself, "I'm not all that happy with the way you look anyway, so you're going to take one for the team." Then, I thought, I would have a beautiful new rack of "perky breasts." How many people do you know can get a boob job at the county's expense? Lol!

After breast surgery, you will have one or more surgical drains in place near your incisions. They are one of the most uncomfortable and inconvenient parts of your post-surgery. I found them to be totally unbearable at first. You have to be extremely careful in making sure you don't pull them out or lay on them.

Make sure that you have someone to help drain them every four hours for the first few days. About a week later, you can drain them every seven hours or so. The amount of fluid will vary from day to day. It is very important that you measure the fluid daily and keep a record of how much blood and waste is being drained. As the volume of fluid decreases, swelling around your surgery site should decrease. Having a surgical drain helps speed up your healing by preventing blood and lymphatic fluid buildup under your skin. You will need to measure the fluid daily, and learn to keep the drain clean. This will help prevent infection. When the fluid volume is 25 CC's or less in a 24-hour period, you can have the drains removed.

My drains stayed in almost three grueling weeks. I was so blessed to have my mother with me. Thank God she is a retired nurse. My mom made sure my drains stayed clean and were draining properly. They literally have to be "milked" to get all of the fluid out the tubes. Remember they are stitched in with one or two little stitches and can be accidently pulled out. Be mindful of that when you shower or bathe. I figured out how to throw them over my shoulder and kept pressing on. I looked forward to the three consecutive days when my drains were at 25 CC's or less.

As the days and weeks went by, I learned how to maneuver my drains; I'd take a pain killer, put on a loose blouse or jacket and do what I do. Two weeks after my surgery, I was hanging out with my good friend, Stevie Wonder, and was the guest speaker for breast cancer prevention at my friend Ms. Mary Parker's church. I later discovered that my friend and Pastor Howard Creesy, Jr. had been pastor there for over 25 years before. My heart was filled with so much joy. I was a walking testimony, determined to show and tell anyone who would listen how great God is to me. That the day I had my drains removed, I had the biggest "Kool-Aid smile ever. Oh Happy Day!!!!!

Flash a Friend

I had no idea what mastectomy breasts looked like. I went to deliver flowers to a dear friend, Doris Creecy, who had recently undergone a double mastectomy. I was a little curious about what to expect, because I was scheduled to have the same surgery in less than two weeks. While I was sitting there asking Doris questions about the procedure, out of nowhere, her Sister Candace says" Show her Doris, show her!" Well, just like that, Doris "Flashed" me her breast. It was a truly hilarious moment for all of us.

Doris gave me a step by step outline of what I could expect from my procedure. In fact, she explained things better to me then my doctor had. I felt so much better about having the procedure. At that point I realized how important it was for me to be aware of what I was getting ready to endure, and that I would offer the same information to another woman who would have to go through Mastectomy.

 I decided that if someone asked me a question about my breasts and were curious about what they looked like, I would pull them to the side and show them. Much to most people's surprise, I got up off the surgery table with about as much as I had when I laid down. In fact, my reconstruction hasn't even begun but my expanders looked really good.

I am so happy that the days of mutilating women and taking the entire breast away are over. Women who are sent home from surgery with a rubber prosthetic are, most times, by the patient's request or due to insurance limitations. If you're curious to know what it looks like before you have it done, don't be afraid to ask to be flashed by a friend.

I believe that it's a great time to have cancer if you get it. Don't be afraid to get a set of new breast, in some situations, you can even get a free "tummy tuck" when the surgeon pushes your stomach fat up to make your new breast. This time you get to choose your desired size and you will always have a gorgeous set of perky girls. Simply stay faithful. Just believe that God has got you and pray that your surgeon knows Him. You will be just fine.

Catching Some Rays

Radiation therapy was a walk in the park compared to chemotherapy. I discovered that it takes more time to find a parking space than it does for your actual radiation treatment. Once your doctor determines that you need radiation, you will have a CT scan that will show the radiologist exactly where your cancer is. The CT scan will take numerous pictures of your affected area. Your radiologist will mark your body with tape, and a black Sharpie. Oh, my God! I'm so happy they don't tattoo anymore. You will wear your markings until your treatments are finished. The length of my radiation treatment was only one minute and 38 seconds. However, I had to be treated the same way every day for 31 days. Close to the end of my radiation treatment, I did get a little tired.

As days went by, I noticed that the skin around my breasts was getting very dark; it was kind of like getting an extreme suntan, which is why I called radiation "catching some rays". As you're going through radiation, make sure you use aloe vera gel (Fruit of the Earth @ Wal-Mart.) It will make an amazing difference in the texture of your skin and with the healing of the radiation burns. I made sure I always had the aloe vera gel with me. If I felt any discomfort, I would pull out my gel and apply it, even if I was at a red light. It made a big difference in the way my skin recovered.

There was only one inconvenience about radiation for me: traveling 50 miles downtown every day for treatment. I was blessed to receive a $100 gas allowance from Avon. There are quite a few companies that will help with daycare, transportation and other items. These organizations are listed in the resource guide at the end of the book.

Gradually my sun burn faded, but the radiated breast is as hard as a brick. Oh well, I can live with that…the optimum word in that statement is "LIVE".

Radiation Machine

Part III—Butterflies

The Magic of God

My dear friend, Stevie Wonder, tells me that his life has been an abundant crusade filled with God's divine evidence of love…magic. God has given him magic through his amazing mother, the late Mrs. Lula Hardaway, through his ten children, his sister, brothers, nieces, nephews and the millions of other people whose lives he has touched and whose lives have touched his.

Having vision without the benefit of sight is something magical that God has bestowed upon Steveland Hardaway Morris. Steve can see through the eyes of his spirit. His true sense of being is totally a supernatural experience. Steve has been a phenomenal friend to me for over 30 years, showing me unconditional love in exceptional ways. We inspire each other in multiple ways. He inspired me to write the book, and I've been the inspiration for at least two songs that he has recorded: "I'm New" and "Sensual Whisper." Both are on his "Conversation Pieces" CD.

Through my cancer journey, Steve was always only a phone call away. He would call me just to say, "I Love You" and was never too busy to share a moment with me. I called him the day I received confirmation that I had cancer. He immediately started telling me to drink alkaline water, and pureed asparagus, informing me that it has tremendous antioxidants that will help fight cancer (Steve is very health conscious). He called me one evening and asked me if I had drunk my asparagus juice. I told him no, and he said, "Go mix it now while I have you on the phone." I got up went to the kitchen and poured the asparagus. I have never tasted anything so nasty in my life! I told Steve it was like drinking a Gecko, not that he knew what a Gecko looked like, but he could hear the disgust in my voice as to what I tasted. I told him I would only drink that nasty stuff if he would call me every day. He had to promise to be my "spoon full of sugar" (to help the medicine/asparagus go down.) Anything that tastes as awful as that has got to be a real cure for anything that might ail you.

Monday mornings were chemo treatment days. One morning, my nurse, Ms. Denise, was prepping me for my drip, and had placed the needle attachment into my port. (Not a pleasant thing, but it's better than burning up the veins in your arms and other common areas. Anyway, Ms. Denise was telling me how beautiful I looked, and how she was always so happy to see me with a brilliant smile and positive attitude. I told her that I was always going to make the best of every situation, and that I get by with a little help from my friends…like Stevie Wonder.

Ms. Denise said, "Stevie Wonder, the entertainer?"

I said, "Yes."

In disbelief, she said, "You're kidding." I said, "Nope. Would you like to speak to him?"

In even more disbelief, she said, "For real?"

This was 8:30 a.m. Atlanta time, 5:30 a.m. Los Angeles time. I dialed his number. He answered and said, "Hey, Sugar."

I said, "Good morning, baby. I'm getting ready to go in to my chemo session. Say hello to my nurse, Ms. Denise."

By this time, Ms. Denise was in extreme disbelief. She said, "You mean the real Stevie Wonder is on the phone?"

I said yes and I passed her my cell phone. Steve said hello to her and told her,

"Please take good care of my dear friend."

Ms. Denise was so excited she couldn't even talk to him. She could not believe what had just happened, nor will she ever forget the day that she received a totally unexpected blessing; she heard him say, "Yes, this is the real Stevie Wonder."

Having him in my life is what I call "the Magic of God," a blessing that only God could have orchestrated through divine intervention, favor, and grace.

A Phenomenal Mother…A Letter from Nadera

My mom has taught me that when fear comes knocking at your door, answer it with unyielding faith. My mother has had to go through a life changing experience within the past year. I will never forget the worst day of my life. It was February 2, 2011, the day my mother was diagnosed with stage IV breast cancer.

I was shocked and scared of what was to come. I would ask myself why. I thought, "I can't lose her; she's all I have. I need her. I need her to see me walk across that stage when I graduate so she can see what God truly blessed her with. I need her whenever I decide to have kids and get married. I need my mom…my life…my best friend…my everything."

She had to have a double mastectomy. She also had to do chemotherapy and radiation treatments. She lost all of her hair and that made her very sad. But my mom never acted like it was a big deal and she didn't want me to worry about it.

I never would have thought my mom, of all people, would have breast cancer. In my eyes, my mom is too strong for anything to get her down. She never let me see her worried or down.

Nothing could ever get the best of her, or so I thought. She never let her fears show on her face. She covered everything with a smile and taught me to do the same.

One thing I greatly admire about her is that even though she has her own problems, she never hesitated to help others and being a blessing to them. My mom has exposed me to a lot of different things. Because of what I learned from her at an early age, I will know exactly what to do when the time comes for me to be independent. I will know to never give up, to let it go and keep it moving, and most importantly, to stay focused.

My mom's life is a great example of what to do when you're determined to survive. Never giving up and knowing that failure is never an option in any circumstance are two valuable lessons I've learned from her. Despite her problems, she never gave up hope. My mom wasn't about to let her problems stand in the way of her ambition. She taught me that although we don't realize it, achieving our goals is worth all the hard work and effort we put forth.

My mom is a very important part of my life: who I am and who I am yet to become. My mom has played a huge role in shaping my personality. I deeply admire her and her qualities. When I grow up, I hope I can be just as good as she is. She is caring, understanding, kind, determined and, of course, **STRONG!** She is a true example of a phenomenal woman.

I love you with all my heart, MOM...Nadera

Nadera & Stevie

When a Smile Shows Up on Its Own

Some days during my daily ritual of chemotherapy, it was sometimes hard looking at myself in the mirror. The following day after my chemotherapy treatments, I would get a "Rosacea" rash under my eyes. It almost looked like I had rosy cheeks. Add to that a bald head, no eyelashes or eyebrows. Looking at myself just wasn't fun during this time.

One day in particular, after having gone through twelve weeks of chemotherapy, I looked in my mirror and immediately saw my father. That wasn't a really bad thing, especially since my dad is still a handsome man at the ripe old age of eighty. Out of his eleven children, I'm the one who is most like him in numerous ways. He says if he had his way, my name would have been Clevette. (Dad's name is Cleveland.)

I took another look in the mirror and, for some reason, I smiled at myself. For the first time in my life, I really saw ME. I mean who I really am. That smile surpassed any level of gorgeousness I had ever experienced on my best day or night out. I saw what I think God sees in me. To see my true beauty and to recognize that hair is only an accessory opens the door to a new realm of self-perception. Ladies, put your best smile on, your earrings, your favorite perfume and keep on stepping.

Raising the Dead!!

During my chemotherapy and other cancer treatment, I was enormously blessed by so many people who showed me so much love, kindness, care, affection, prayer, and many other gestures of their love. I was lying in my bed. It was on a Friday, and I was feeling pretty bad.

With symptoms of the chemo lingering in my body, I was tired,

I was nauseous, my body was aching, my mouth was hurting, and my hair, of course, was coming out.

I was feeling down in the dumps because of my symptoms, but I was even sadder, knowing that I had not heard from Steve all week. Just hearing his ring tone, "I Just Called to Say I Love You" would put a huge smile on my face and a song in my heart. This particular day, I was laying there watching my 10th episode of "House." Having never watched the show before cancer, I guess I could relate to many of the story lines. So, again, as I lay there watching TV not feeling good, my mom came upstairs and brought me something to eat. She said, "Baby, are you okay?" I said, "Mom, I'm not doing so good." This may have been about 1:00 pm. About 4:30 that afternoon, I heard that very special ringtone. I sat straight up in my bed. It was like I had been struck by lightning. I answered the phone.

It was Steve; he said "hey sweetie, what are you doing?"

I said, in a really happy voice, "Oh just laying here watching TV."

He asked me how far I lived from the airport and that he was going to come and see me. I was standing straight up by now.

He said, "I am leaving the Carter Center now. I'll call you as I get closer to the airport."

I ran downstairs screaming to my mom, "Steve is coming to see me!" I was running around like a crazy woman. "Steve's coming to see me!"

She said, "Oh, my! I should change your name to Lazarus because that phone call was like Jesus raising the dead!" All she could do was laugh at how excited I was. Just hearing his voice made me jump out of bed and get moving. Talk about good medicine!!!

About ten minutes later, he called back and said, "Can you get up and come to the airport? I've got to leave, but I have something for Nadera." By this time, I was almost dressed. I said, "I'm on my way." You would have thought that I had an infusion of extreme adrenaline through my entire body. I jumped in the car, drove to the airport, parked in the garage and just waited for him to come.

I propped myself on top of a large flower planter, swinging my feet and drinking my alkaline water. Like a little kid waiting to see "Santa Claus". Again...I was a happy girl.

When Steve's driver pulled up in a Black Navigator, I jumped down off the planter and I walked over and got into the car. As always, he greeted me with a hug and a kiss and said, "It's so good to see you." It is always so good to see him, too. We didn't have a lot of time. He was rushing for his flight to get back to Los Angeles. He reached in his bag and pulled out two boxes: A Mac notebook for Nadera and an iPad for me. Talk about being blessed and knowing that God is truly in the blessing business. At that time, neither one of us knew that I was going to write a book. As God would have it, Steve knew I had a story to tell, so he made sure I had a fantastic tool in order to write this wonderful story that would be a blessing to so many people. I understand firsthand what Steve meant when he sang the song, *"That's what Friends are for. In good times and bad times, I'll be on your side forever more. That's what friends are for."*

Getting Some Ms. Bunny Love

One must show himself friendly to be a friend. You can never have too many friends, and I have been so very fortunate all of my life. Over the years, I have made great choices as to whom I called "friend." I have been blessed all my life and have been fortunate enough to surround myself with likeminded and like-spirited people.

A sweet and dear lady whom I call friend is Ms. Bunny. She is a retired flight attendant for Delta Air Lines and she has the most amazing smile I've ever seen. When she walks into a room, you will notice her immediately. Her bright red lipstick, pearly white teeth, shimmering hair and her jazzy walk all set her apart. When Ms. Bunny smiles at you; you know you have surely been smiled at.

Having experienced three pulmonary embolisms in less than two years, not to mention some other health issues lets you know how blessed and special Ms. Bunny is. It is truly a miracle that she is still here with us. Yet, she's another survivor that keeps a positive attitude and surrounds herself with likeminded and like-spirited people. With the love, care and support of her husband, Ron, she is forever evolving into a more dynamic woman every day. They have been married for over twenty-five years and have been together for almost forty years. I call them Ron and Bunny Love.

Ms. Bunny is a woman who knows her way around a kitchen. She owns and manages her own catering company. Whether preparing meals for an intimate dinner for two or creating an enchanting culinary display for a few hundred people attending a huge party, she shines. When I was going through my treatment, I didn't have a very big appetite, but I did want comfort food.

I would ask Ms. Bunny to bring me mashed potatoes and gravy.

Not only did she bring the mashed potatoes and gravy, but she also brought me baked chicken that brought me to tears. Plus, she had baked a "slap your mama in the face" sweet potato pie. On another occasion, Ms. Bunny prepared a huge piece of salmon. It was broiled to perfection, with pasta salad extraordinaire, cookies for dessert and sweet tea to drink. She topped it off with that big beautiful smile just for me.

She is another angel that God has put into my life. She was always there for me; just a phone call away. She and Ron would take me to my treatments or to my doctors' appointments whenever I needed them. Ms. Bunny and Ron would never be too busy to lend a helping hand just for me.

Having great friends in your life like Ms. Bunny and Ron really made my treatments a lot more bearable. There is not a week that goes by that I don't get me some Ron and Bunny Love.

Where Is the Finish Line?

Another reason why I wanted to write this book was because of a dream I had. After my chemotherapy was completed, I just knew that I was finished with my treatment and that I was cancer free. I had no idea that I was going to have to endure a double mastectomy or radiation.

My oncologist never once mentioned any additional treatment after my chemotherapy. So, in my dream, I am running a marathon. I'm running and running and running. After my last mile, I see people standing all over the route cheering me on, being very supportive and just happy that I am on my journey to completing this marathon. As I was going up the hill then down another hill then around a curve I can see the finish line. I was feeling what my ex-husband used to call "the runner's high." I was feeling really good. Then my adrenaline kicked in and I was feeling even better. I'm saying to myself, "I'm at the finish line." I can see it; I can feel it. I see the balloons before me and more people cheering me on. The finish line sign is right before me.

As I was running, I started to see the people disappear and I saw the finish line disappear as well. The balloons started floating away into the sky, and   I got to what I thought was the finish line, and there was a little old lady standing there. I asked her where the finish line was. I told her I had seen it when I was running around the corner and that when I was going up and down the hill. I could see it in the distance. What happened to it? With these beautiful, grandma eyes, she smiled at me and handed me a bottle of water. She then gave me a hug and said, "Baby, they moved the finish line."

"They moved it?" I said.

The little lady responded and said, "Sweetie, they moved it because you still have a little ways to go."

I said, "A little more ways to go? How can it be? I thought I was finished."

The little lady said, "I understand what you're saying; but, sweetie, you have to go a little further. You are going to get to the finish line. Just take this water and a short break." She continued, "Get back out there and run. Never lose sight of that finish line; just keep it moving. Don't stop, and don't second guess yourself. Just keep going and I guarantee you will get to the end of the finish line."

In total disbelief, I started running at a very slow pace, but as I continued to move along, I was excited to see the people coming back to the sidelines. And, again, they started cheering me on. As I looked in the very far distance, I could see the balloons high above the trees. I kept running and running and running, and then I finally came down the hill and saw that finish line again.

It took me a lot longer than I thought it should have. I had to go through some bad weather. I got a really bad sunburn, and I had to go through some really horrific storms. I was cut by falling debris. It really was a very strenuous journey. I kept it moving and I stayed positive. When I finally got to the end of that marathon, I was reunited with all of the people who love and care about me. All the people who were there for me, giving me support and kind thoughts along the way: those were the ones who were there to pick me up when I fell to my knees at the finish line. They helped me cross over a winner.

I shared that dream to remind you not to get discouraged when you think that the finish line is right in front of you and somebody moved it. Just know that if you dig down into your heart of hearts, the courage will come and you can complete the task.

You will be cured and you will be free of cancer. Most of all, the confidence that you gain through your journey is something no one could ever have given to you. You had to go through all of that crazy stuff to get your reward. The old saying about picking yourself up by your bootstraps, lacing them up, dusting yourself off and getting back out there and doing it again is solid advice. When you believe, you will achieve. It is so easy to give in to your fears, but you can't get through the rain without getting wet. Just keep on going and hold on. Don't be afraid; there's nothing to fear. There is truly a miracle waiting for you at the end of the finish line.

Family Praise Report

I am so blessed to have an amazing family. My brother (Cleveland) and mother (Angloria) live in San Antonio, Texas. I have two sisters (Gail and Debbie) and uncles (Douglas and Arnold) two aunts (Geraldine and Jean) in Baltimore, Maryland. My father, (Cleveland) and three sisters (Renee, Van, and Lisa) and brother (Kenny) are in North Carolina. And then I have a host of other friends who love me all over the country.

While I was going through treatment, it was quite difficult to keep everyone informed. All of my family and many of my friends wanted to know how I was progressing on a weekly basis.

During weeks of chemotherapy, it was very difficult to communicate with anyone. I wouldn't talk to the family or friends for a while. When I felt better, I would tell one family member, then that family member would tell another family member. Sometimes, the other family member would get upset. Then the other family member would not relay the information correctly.

During the same time, my brother was diagnosed with a tumor in his brain. He and I have always been very close, so we talked every day. However, the rest of the family wasn't happy

94

because they wanted to know what was going on with us.

Finally, I came up with the idea that maybe we could do a weekly conference call. That way, we could keep everyone informed and not have to relay the information over and over and over again.

When I had something to tell them about my diagnosis, I would make a phone call to, first, my brother. He would call my sister, my mom and my dad. At the same time, I would be getting five people on my line. My niece, Nikiya, who is very adept at working her cell phone, would get another five family members on the phone. Before we knew it, there would be almost twenty of us talking, or should I say laughing, at one time. In order for all of us to hear and be heard, we did have to lay down some rules. The rules went like this: I would make the first introduction because the call was mostly about me. Everyone on the call had to be quiet until I finished saying what I had to say. After I would discuss all the things I needed to talk about, the family took turns asking me questions I would then answer. After the important information was discussed and all of their questions had been answered, the celebrating would start. We would all gather our cocktails of choice. Most times, we would just toast to the good news that I would have just told them.

We would get a spoon and ting our glasses like we were in the room with each other.

These conference calls ended up being the highlights of our day every week for nineteen weeks.

Not only did they get to hear what was going on with me, but we all got to hear what was going on with each other, which brought us much closer as a family.

Having a strong foundation of family values from my grandmother, Annie Bell Pennick, we always shared love, food, laughter and great times together. My grandmother transitioned in 2000.

We still laugh, love and have a great time at our family reunions and holidays. While I was having a conversation with my friend, Stevie Wonder, I told him about the conference call and how much fun we have.

He was so excited to hear about what we were doing that he insisted on being on the next call.

I mentioned to him that I was going to have my mastectomy in a few days. I told him that I would have a conference call with him and the family after my surgery. Steve said, "No, let's have a conference call the night before you go in for surgery."

I said, "That's a fantastic idea. Sure, we will do that." The Sunday night before my surgery (September 24, 2011) with my mother and father sitting in my living room with me, I called my brother, my sisters, Gail and Debbie and my uncle Hunka. I tried to call my sister, Renee, but she didn't answer. (You know she wasn't happy about missing the call.) I told the family before the call started that we were going to have a new person join the call that night. They were all totally blown away when I told them that Steve was going to be on the call. I explained to them that Steve had a three- to five-second delay in responding to a statement.

I suggested that they speak and give him a moment to gather what was said and then he would respond. I put everyone on hold and called Steve who was the next voice they heard on the line. I introduced him to everyone and everyone said hello.

My uncle Douglas, who is the same age as Steve, proceeded to tell Steve how proud he was of him. At ten years old, he released a song called "Hey Harmonica Man" that he really liked. Steve responded by saying every artist has a song that they love or they hate, or that they wished they had never recorded. "Hey Harmonica Man" happened to be the song that Steve absolutely hated! Oh, my God! It was the funniest thing. We all laughed. Uncle Doug was so surprised to hear such a response. Steve had a conversation with everyone, answering questions, and making small talk. We laughed and joked a little bit more. Then Steve got very serious. He wanted to take a little time to tell them how much he loved me, how much he cared about me, how important it was for him to let my family know that I was important to him and that we were important to him as a family. He then began to say a prayer for me. He prayed for my family.

He prayed for my health. He prayed for me to be cured of my cancer. My father couldn't believe that he was on the phone with Stevie Wonder. He was so amazed at how sincere and how much Steve really cared about me. We all laughed a little bit longer, and then Steve had to get off the phone. We are all so grateful that he had taken the time to share with me, and to have just called to say, "I Love You".

Late Night Buddha

Exactly twelve days after my double mastectomy, my dear friend, Stevie Wonder, was visiting Atlanta and was performing in concert for the birthday of civil rights leader Dr. Joseph Lowery. Rev. Lowery was celebrating his 90th birthday at the Woodruff Arts Center at the High Museum. Steve had promised me during the conference call that when he came to town in a few weeks, he would see me. He called me early that morning before he left Los Angeles and told me to rest all day that Sunday because he wanted me to come to the show that night. I told him I would absolutely get my rest so that I could hang out with him at the show.

I wasn't in a great deal of pain at that point; I just had to move very slowly. About 7:00 p.m. that evening Steve called and said for me to start heading to the venue. My big sister, Gail, was visiting me that weekend and, of course, Lynn was there. The three of us jumped in the car and went down to the High Museum.

When we pulled up at the artist entrance, this guy yelled in the window and asked, "Hey, is Stevie Flowers in this car?"

I said, "Yes."

"Here's a parking space right here. Come on in," he said.

Now, that's what I call VIP treatment! We were escorted to the backstage area. Steve was getting ready to go on to sing "Happy Birthday" to Dr. Lowery.

We were hanging out backstage with Rev. Al Sharpton, India Arie, Peabo Bryson, and Cicely Tyson. After the show was over, we went to Steve's dressing room. We sat down, talked and told jokes. Time was getting pretty late; it was around midnight. Steve said he was hungry and wanted all of us to go have dinner together. After 11:00 on Sunday night, there's really no place to eat in downtown Atlanta. The only place I could think of was a little Chinese restaurant called Buddha.

The restaurant was less than ten minutes away from where we were. Steve's security team was a little concerned about the layout of the place. When we got there, his security people went in first. They saw that there was a place where we could sit that would be blocked by some plants.

There were only about ten people with us. As we sat and enjoyed our dinner, no one even attempted to come and invade our space. We all laughed and enjoyed each other's company. Steve was so happy to see me, and the fact that I was actually up and out twelve days after my double mastectomy surgery made it all the more special. At the end of the evening, we were all getting ready to go. The servers who work at the restaurant asked if they could take pictures with Steve. He said yes and, let a few of the patrons in the restaurant take pictures with him as well; he is just that kind of guy. I was so happy to have the opportunity to spend the evening with my dear friend and I was so grateful that I was feeling well enough to attend. As always, God works everything out for my good. I know that I am truly blessed.

Jimmy Choo Shoes

I have been very fortunate to have made so many delightful friends in my life. One is a really sweet lady named Beverly. Beverly is like no other woman I've ever met. She is a charmingly beautiful woman; very attractive, very smart and extremely personable. She is lovely in every way. During my journey, Beverly would call and make sure I was doing okay. Having gone through breast cancer with her sister Precious, she understood all that I was going through.

While I was working through my last few radiation treatments in the month of December (2011), Beverly called and said she had a ticket for me join her at Piedmont Golf Club. It was a fundraiser for an organization called Atlanta Victim Assistance, which is headed by another dynamic woman by the name of Brenda Muhammad. This was a very nice and extremely elegant reception held to raise money for people who are the victims of violent crime and their families. They had a silent auction with a fantastic collection of shoes that had been donated by the likes of Michael Jordan, Magic Johnson, Jasmine Guy, Jennifer Holliday and many other stars, entertainers and athletes. While I was waiting for a friend of mine to finish a conversation with someone else, I decided to take a look at some of the shoes that were on display for the silent auction. My friend was trying on the pair of Jimmy Choo shoes. Unfortunately, they did not fit her.

I walked over to the table where my friend, Beverly, said, "Stevie, try the shoes on."

I said, "I am not trying on these shoes. They are $250 and I know I can't afford to buy them."

Beverly responded by saying, "Don't worry about that. Just try the shoes on." It was like a Cinderella moment when I tried on the shoes; they fit! (Keep in mind that I had no clue what a Jimmy Choo shoe was.) The shoes had been given to the organization by the singer, Jennifer Holliday.

Jennifer Holliday was one of the original Dream Girls from the Broadway play of the same name. The shoes that I tried on were the actual shoes that she wore in the play some twenty years ago. The shoes retail for $700. When I put the shoes on people started taking pictures and gathered around me.

Beverly said, "You have to have those shoes."

Again, I told her that I could not afford the shoes.

She said, "It doesn't matter, Stevie. You are going to have these shoes. I am going to pay for them and give them to you as your breast cancer survivor gift."

I could not believe it. This was one of those amazing moments that God orchestrated specifically for me. When things are in "Divine Order" in your life, God blesses you as long as He knows that you put Him first.

What an unexpected blessing from an extremely dear friend. Thank you so much, Beverly for being you and only you.

The Trumpet Awards

The foundation for success in businesses is networking, networking, and networking. I moved to Atlanta in 2006 expecting to have great success with my florist and event planning business as I had in Los Angeles. Unfortunately, it didn't happen quite the way I planned. Still, as time has gone on, I have experienced growth and success in my business.

In October of 2010, I became a volunteer event coordinator and greeter for the Atlanta Business League.

Meeting people and helping to make magic happen at events is what I love to do. In doing so, I have had the wonderful opportunity to meet and greet a lot of business owners and mentors.

One of my mentors, Ms. Mary Parker, asked me to take a presentation bouquet to an amazing woman, Mrs. Xernona Clayton, who is the founder and creator of the Trumpet Awards. I had been trying to meet Ms. Clayton since I moved to Atlanta, but I just never had the opportunity. I was blessed to have the opportunity to present a fabulous bouquet of flowers to Ms. Clayton the day that the City of Atlanta named a street and park after her. Ms. Clayton was so pleased and happy with the impressive bouquet that she welcomed me to come to her office and design the flowers in vases for her. Unfortunately, she had to leave town on short notice, and I was not able to design the flowers for her.

About two weeks later, I contacted Mrs. Clayton's assistant Maria (also a breast cancer survivor) who suggested that I bring floral samples to show Ms. Clayton. She loved the flowers and my ideas, so she gave me the contract. It was just that simple. In fact, just four days after having 31 radiation treatments, I started placing flowers on tables for The Trumpet Awards.

The flowers and all of the event décor were simply gorgeous. They were liked by all who attended. In fact, one of the most well-connected gentlemen in Atlanta, Mr. Thomas Dortch, Jr., was so impressed with the setup that he has hired me to decorate events for many of the organizations he is associated with. I'm speaking of divine order at its best.

Westley Chasing Angels

Researchers say some animals can tell when you are sick. I have learned from my experience with my purebred who I adopted almost four years ago. His name is Wesley. It's funny because a group of children found him on a street called Wesley Chapel Road, so they named him Wesley. As an older dog, he's very laid back; and quiet. His main concern is making sure he can always see me.

When I started my chemotherapy, it looked like he knew that I would have had a treatment that day. Wesley would lie on the floor next to my bed in his bed, and then he would come to check on me. He would go back and lie down and never leave my side. He was so attentive to me that he would never even go downstairs to eat or use the restroom. My daughter would have to make him go relieve himself. It got to the point that we would bring his food upstairs because he never wanted to be far away from me. I thought it was simply amazing. Being a very old dog, he was more like a geriatric old man. He slept all day. He got his rest and played a little bit with toys. But, for the most part, he looked after and watched over me. Some days when I was not able to move very much, he was always there to keep me company and just watched over me.

After I finished my chemotherapy treatment, I went to see my medical oncologist. He said that my PET scan results had come back and the results were magnificent. My body had responded so well to chemotherapy that there was little or no trace of the cancer left in my lymph nodes or outside my breasts. I came home so excited and happy I called the family for a conference call. We had a very exciting call and then I went to sleep. The very next morning, Wesley was running around my bed jumping up and down barking. I was wondering, "What is wrong with this crazy dog?"

But then I realized that dogs can smell cancer and the fact that
103

my PET scan showed that my cancer was gone, he was singing with the angels. It was an amazing thing to see and hear. For about fifteen minutes, he was just jumping on the bed. He never barks in the house, but he was barking that particular morning. All I can say is I received notice that my cancer was gone and my dog confirmed it! I didn't need a Saint Bernard to bring me whiskey on a mountain top. I simply needed a little guy name Wesley to let me know the Big Guy had worked it out.

Oprah Calling

Every so often, opportunities just seem to fall in my lap. While I was at work one day, a lady called and asked if a film crew for the Oprah network could use the building where I work as a place to film a community meeting. About a week later the producers for the reality show stopped by to take a look. They absolutely loved the space; the contract was signed.

As they were leaving, one of the producers named John (who

had the coolest British accent) asked me, "How do you feel about disrespectful children mistreating their mother?"

I responded and said, "I can show you better than I can tell you. Go ask my daughter, Nadera. She is standing over there."

Nadera was in the middle of directing a scene for her history film project. I introduced Nadera to John, who immediately smiled and shook her hand. In the same instant, he asked her, "How do you feel about disrespectful children mistreating their mother?"

Nadera began to tear up, and started telling how she felt when I was diagnosed with cancer. Nadera told John that not too long ago, she was going through a rebellious stage where she thought she was grown and that world only revolved around her. She remembered the fact that she was always selfishly thinking about herself and no one else. She wouldn't do her chores when I would ask her; she was just being disrespectful on all accounts.

I was amazed when she told John that she took my kindness and patience for granted, thinking that I was always going to do for her and cater to her needs. But that all changed with my diagnosis. Nadera then found herself dealing with the most terrifying thing in her life.

John saw the tears in her eyes and Nadera began to tell him about the changes she had made in her attitude, how much she loved and needed to show me respect and have a more cooperative attitude.

He felt that she was very sincere about making sure she treated me better, and that she could be a very positive influence on the two young ladies that were going to be on this reality show.

The next day, I got a call from the production assistant who told me that they were rewriting the script to include me and Nadera. John was so impressed with both of us that he changed the dynamic of the show. His new goal was to help these two sisters see how important it is to be respectful and kind to your mom.

We were in production for almost three weeks, filming at various locations around the city. I even took the two sisters to a children's shelter, where they could see and meet teens living through hardships without their mothers and family.

By the third week of taping, the girls were being more respectful to their mom. They also had a much different outlook on how valuable she was to them. I explained to them, "You only get one mother and once she's gone, she's gone for good. Don't wait until you are losing her to appreciate her." Maybe one-day *Bee Stings, Bumble Bees & Butterflies* will appear on Oprah's book club list. The Power of Positive Thinking really works.

I'm a Survivor!!!!!

I have always regarded myself as a survivor. From being born premature and weighing just three pounds at birth in 1959, to being homeless with a nine-month old baby, to moving from Maryland to California to save my life, to moving from Washington state to rebuild my life, to settling in Atlanta, Georgia during a time the economy went bust, to surviving the loss of a successful business of twenty-two years.

I've gone through some really traumatic circumstances, Yet Still I Rise!!!!!!

I have been an advocate for helping survivors of breast cancer in numerous ways, from donating flowers to survivors during breast cancer month; brightening the days of women who were getting mammograms by giving them beautiful orchids; to helping my friend Linda Taylor salute survivors on the Classic Soul Cruise by making Queen of Courage sashes and presentation bouquets.

However, until you have visited and sat in the chemo chair with a chemo drip in your veins, you don't really know what it is. Until you've had your breast tissue surgically removed in the form of a mastectomy or a lumpectomy, you don't know what it is. Until you have laid on the table and have that wonderful radiation machine circle your body (in a figure eight motion), you don't know what it is.

Until the day that you look in the mirror and are missing a major accessory; what happened to my hair? You don't know what it is to be a survivor.

Survivorship is not to be taken lightly. It is a badge of honor that we carry and are reminded of every day of our lives. As survivors, we fight the good fight; some of us don't make it. Still, many of us do. We fight until we can't fight it any longer. So, when you meet someone who tells you they are a survivor, make sure you give them a big smile and a hug. Say a prayer to God and ask that they continue to be healed. Remember, survivors are God's miracles. They are making believers out of all who know us, love us and gain strength when they see us. I truly am a Survivor!!!

The Man in Black

One day, I stopped by to see another fantastic lady, my friend, Carol, who works for the Atlanta Hawks. Carol had not seen me since I had finished my chemotherapy surgery, and had just finished my radiation. While catching her up on things, she said, "We need to get you to a game."

The next Wednesday, the Hawks played the Golden State Warriors. My daughter, Nadera, Lynn, coworker, Whitney and I went to the game.

I put on my black stretch pants, my black boots and a cute little top. I was feeling quite good that night! I saw this man sitting, looking at his phone and texting; I said to myself; "He's handsome." He was sitting near the French fry counter, so I decided to go get some French fries. I got in line to get my French fries with my daughter and, when I turned around, the man in black was standing there very close to me. He said "hello" I said "hello" back.

As we conversed, I caught him totally off guard because he didn't expect me to respond with a big bright smile.

As we talked, I discovered that, his mother is a breast cancer survivor. She has written a book; he's working on making it into a screenplay. And most important...he was very single.

A dynamic example of being at the right place at the right time! Since then, we have definitely talked a lot more. He and I are collaborating on this book and some other projects.

I'm not afraid of my inner Butterfly…

I'm Cancer Free!

When you are going through cancer treatment, you sometimes wonder, "Will I ever be cancer free?" Like most things, freedom is in your mind. As I have recovered from all the treatment that I've gone through, people ask me, "Are you in remission?"

I ask them, "What is remission? What is that? I have no clue. All I know is that I am cancer free and God spared my life." You cannot doubt God's favor, your ability to have grace and your need to remain faithful.

If you are determined to be cancer free, you have to know it, live it, think it, feel it and wholeheartedly believe it.

Once you have that PET scan after your treatment and your doctor tells you that all traces of your cancer are gone, understand that you're blessed. To find out that you don't have to take any type of medication in terms of estrogen blockers or other things is truly a blessing. All I can say is, "I serve a mighty God who has totally healed my body.

It doesn't hurt that I'm always a confident optimist that if you give me lemons I'm going to make a lemon drop martini.

People look at me and say how they would never know that I've gone through as much as I've gone through in fact I've been told many times that I look like I'm "Glowing." If I didn't tell you that I was a stage IV breast cancer survivor you would never know. I really don't think I've ever felt better. I've never been happier in my, nor have I ever felt so liberated in my life.

Now, I feel that there's nothing I can't do, that there is no project I can't accomplish, and most of all, there's no way that I can be any better than I am today. I am a better woman today, a stronger woman today, a more determined woman today and a more liberated woman today than I've ever been in my life. I am totally at peace in every aspect of my life. I'm living life every day to the fullest.

I am so grateful to be a survivor and to know that I am and will remain cancer free. I am healed by His stripes. God has given me an awesome testimony to share with all who choose to listen. I thank you Lord for giving people ears to hear.

Life More Abundantly

The Bible says in John 10:10, "Jesus came that we might have life, and that we might have it more abundantly." If we just honor the Word of God and stay true to Him and His Word, we would know that when the Lord said we might have abundant life, it didn't mean that we're going to have life without trials and tribulation, all of the body parts we were born with. We may have to figure out how to have an abundant life without breasts, without hands, without feet or maybe even without having the use of our eyes and ears. But we still have life!

The key to make the best of every situation we're in. Claim 'your' victory over negative issues you are faced with. Always remain positive and know that God has your back.

Glory Flower & Three Butterflies

Writing this book has caused me a lot of anxiety. Attempting to stay on task for the ever- changing deadlines has not been easy. As my good friend, Stevie Wonder, said in the foreword, this book is my "baby." Oh, my God! I had to feed it, change it, stay up all night with it and, most of all, love and nurture it.

I finally figured out why I wasn't supposed to have this baby prematurely. I wasn't finished by any stretch of the imagination. There was a divine timeline that I wasn't aware of. I was supposed to meet a group of women who would all be godmothers to my baby. It would be a dynamic group of cancer survivors who came together for an amazing pre-ordained event.

God has surrounded me with likeminded and like-spirited people all of my life. Just when I thought I couldn't meet another sweet spirited, caring, giving, kindhearted, loving Proverbs 31 woman adored by her husband and children, Lady Regina and her anointed crew, the Sisters of Substance, came into my life. I have never seen anyone so generous with their time, talents and resources.

I received an invitation to Pretty in Pink; it would be a celebration in my honor. I immediately replied to such a sweet gesture by offering to donate ten centerpieces. While on the phone with Lady Knight, I asked her, "Do I know you?"

She replied and said, "We've never met, but I know your spirit." Her voice was so very familiar. It was like the voice of an angel that I had heard before. We became sisters in Christ immediately.

The week before the event, I visited Lady Knight at her home to see what I could do to help with decorations. Much to my surprise, there was absolutely nothing she would allow me to do. When I saw all that she had already done, it brought tears of joy to my eyes. Talk about pretty and pink: all her centerpieces were ready, the gift bags were stuffed, and the China, stemware and flatware were already in place. I could only smile and be happy for being blessed enough to have been chosen to take part in this amazing event. Little did I know that I was just one small piece of the puzzle that would comprise this glory-filled occasion.

This very special day was met with awesome weather, something that Lady Knight had been praying for daily. God saw fit to show up and show out all through the day. In fact, over twenty-five breast cancer survivors were being celebrated and all of us were, first, giving honor to God for saving our lives.

When I drove up to the property, I could see this huge breast cancer ribbon on the front lawn. Wow! About the same time, a young man walked up to my car door welcoming me while taking my car to the valet parking area. Oh my! I knew I was in for a treat when I saw an enormous tent filled with white folding chairs tied with pink sashes

There were rose petals streaming down the aisle and four tables filled with flowers and gifts. It looked like something that you would see on Lifestyles of the Rich and Famous. "All of this is for me because I survived breast cancer?" I thought. I could hardly believe my eyes. I had been truly blessed by a total stranger who simply was obedient to the spirit of God.

The grand home was set up with five eating areas, both inside and outside, with seating for over one hundred people. There where black chair covers, again with pink ties, elegant table linens and place settings. We were escorted to our tables by a member from the Sisters of Substance team. These ladies gladly offered us service with a smile, kindness beyond measure, and they were willing to address our every need or desire. I really felt like a queen for the day. I'm sure all of the other survivors felt the same way.

Lady Knight asked if I would share an excerpt from the book entitled, "The Butterfly." She introduced me to the audience by calling me "Glory Flower" (which I thought that was pretty cool.) I happily obliged her and began to share the passage with the group. As I began to read about the transformation of the caterpillar becoming a beautiful, breathtaking butterfly, three butterflies flew into the tent. They were flying all over the ceiling of the tent for all to see. It was one of those divine moments that gave us all confirmation that we were all on one accord and were all in store for a phenomenal afternoon filled with God's grace, favor and love.

The afternoon progressed with exquisite food, great music, awesome testimonies, praise dancing and poetry. We prayed for and were anointed with fragrant oil. I realized that this was a very special gathering of women who had experienced the Bee Sting of cancer and were put in this space, at this time, to support each other in the struggle of survivorship.

Thank you all for your love and care especially, Bishop and Lady Knight.

The Upper Deck

Sunday, May 24, 2013 was the date of my daughter Nadera graduated from high school...a day that was a miracle that GOD made happen for both of us.
Nadera had asked her Godfather Stevie Wonder to come to her graduation, months ahead of time. I am simply amazed at how he still has the energy to keep up with all of the extensive demands on his time. Remember he is a

113

father, brother, uncle, boss, producer, writer, arranger, and has a girlfriend half his age…Men all over the world might want to drink "Wonder Juice" if it were available (lol).

Unfortunately, Steve was late leaving Los Angeles and was not able to check his luggage. He could have taken the next flight with his luggage, but would have missed Nadera's graduation. With the clothes on his back, and his carry-on, he got on the flight. Steve called me around 8:00 a.m. He was at the airport, but needed to check into the hotel. I had made reservations with the general manager at the Sheraton Atlanta. He had given me the family rate on two presidential suites, with a smaller suit in the middle of them for my mom.

By the time Steve arrived at the Georgia Dome, the graduation had already begun. I had been in touch with the dome security to make arrangements for my mom who was in a wheelchair, and the rest of the family and friends to enter through the artist entrance. A very nice young man met us and took us to our seats.

Steve's handler, Francis called me and said that Steve didn't want to be a distraction during the ceremony. I said, "No worries, I can fix that". I called the security guard and told him the situation. He escorted all ten of us down to the garage where Steve was waiting. I asked if we could sit in the upper deck and we were immediately taken to that location. It was the perfect place to watch our baby girl walk across the stage. I can't tell you the joy that was in my heart. Steve and I sat next to each other eating skittles, and starburst. We both had sugar rushes (lol).

After the graduation, we took the elevator down to the holding area for the graduates, and that's when the fun started. When the elevator door opened, there was a woman standing there who lost it. "Oh My God", "Oh My God", she screamed, Steve took a picture with her. Nadera's math teaching who knew that Steve was her God father, ran to where she was yelling, "Nadera your God father is really here." It was hilarious to see how crazy people act when they are in his company...STEVIE WONDER!!!

Steve wanted to meet the valedictorian of the class and he took lots of photos with many of the graduates. Certainly, that was a day they will never forget.

I had made dinner reservations for us at McCormick & Schmitt located in the CNN building downtown Atlanta. We got there very early and when the hostess saw on the reservation notes that I had requested a table in the back, she gave us their private room. I later found out that she did that because she was touched by how attentive I was to my mother. It was a wonderful evening of food, fun and laughter. As always...God is always showing me how much he loves me and he truly gives me the desires of my heart. An incredible day that none of us will ever forget.

Steve & Nadera

Nipple Envy

December 30th, 2011 was one of the HAPPIEST days of my life. That was the last day of cancer treatment. In eight months I had experienced twenty-five rounds of chemotherapy, a bilateral mastectomy, and thirty-one consecutive days of radiation therapy. Oh my!!! I was a happy girl coming into the New Year.

You'll never know how elated I was that night. I was happy that my treatment was finally over, and that my prognosis of being cancer free was outstanding. I danced into the New Year of 2012 Cancer Free, Treatment Free, and Cancer Drug Free.

Having reconstructive surgery is a very personal and individual endeavor. It varies according to what your specific ideas are regarding your body. I chose to wait almost a year after my mastectomy to start my reconstruction journey.

Some women decide to have their reconstruction surgery within weeks of their mastectomy. Unfortunately, this sometimes can prove to be disastrous.

The body needs time to heal from all of the stress of surgery, chemotherapy, and radiation therapy that you have endured as a result of your cancer.

In December of 2013, I scheduled my surgery to have my expanders replaced with my new permanent breast implants. I didn't want to increase my breast size, as was the joke from my male friends... "Why don't you get a couple double D's?" My response was simply that I prefer not to walk around with the weight of two-liter soda bottles on my chest.

As I prepared for the surgery that I thought would make me totally whole and complete again, my attitude was positive as usual. This surgery was a lot easier, and simpler than I expected no complications at all. The surgery took about an hour and a half and I was on my way home. I didn't have any drains to deal with, and very little pain or inflammation.

Dr. Losken, my cosmetic oncologist took a little fat from my stomach, to fill a small air pocket that was in my left breast as a result of the first surgery.

Three months later I returned to see Dr. Losken to have my nipples built. I know that sounds strange, but; he sliced the skin on where my nipple would have been, and then stitched it into the shape of a small nipple. He did this on each breast. I never knew how much I missed my nipples until I got them back. Unfortunately, within four months, the skin that the nipple was made of settled, and my nipples were then flat. I was a little disappointed about the nipple collapse, but ever so grateful to still be alive.

Two months later, I had the very last part of my breast reconstruction. This was the day that I would have the Areola tattooed on my breast. I called it, "having my head lights turned on."

I had an appointment with a registered nurse who was trained in Areola tattooing. I've never had the desire to be tattooed, and didn't quite know what to expect. Fortunately, my left breast was still numb from radiation and mastectomy so I felt very little pressure from the needle pressing into my skin.

The right breast on the other had a different feeling all together. OMG, the skin on my breast that had not been radiated; therefore, it had a lot more sensitivity. For me it was quite uncomfortable. I will never understand why people, especially women say they really enjoy it. I guess I'm just not where they are!

I was given a cute little bag with some extra gauze, and tape. The very nice tattoo nurse told me to put Lubriderm lotion on it, and to change the bandages the next morning.

I got up early the next day and went to the store. When I returned home, I found that blood had saturated the gauze and was dripping down my stomach. When I tried to pull off the gauze, it was stuck to my skin. This wasn't pleasant at all. When I finally got the gauze off, I could see that the tattooed areola was blistered and inflamed. The tattooing didn't look like it had covered the space very well. It reminded me of the time when I fell off my sister Debbie's bike and tore up both of my knee caps. That's what my breasts looked like…two scuffed knees. They look better now, however I have accepted the fact that my breast will NEVER look the way they use to. That reality is ever present, however; my breasts have never defined who I am as a person, or what I am as a "Totally Complete Woman". I'm Still PHAT! (Pretty Hot and Tempting)

Never Happier

All I can say is that I serve a Mighty God! In the past five years I've been blessed to accomplish some amazing achievements.

Anyone who knows me will tell you that, when you ask me "how are you", I always say "FANTASTIC". Every day I am truly FANTASTIC. I can honestly say that I have never been happier in my life. I've enjoyed numerous life altering events in my Fifty-Six years on this earth.

I am so grateful for every moment that I have lived, even though the pain of cancer, the untimely death of my dear mother, as a result of negligence at a hospital I trusted, and the passing of my sweet little dog Wesley the same week. I even had to sell my Corvette!!! I wasn't happy at all.

God kept me, and gave me perfect peace. I prayed for the strength of my great, great, great, great, great grandmothers that week; my female ancestors who suffered, through tremendous hardships and struggles. They lived in a time when they were taken from their home land Africa, and bought here to America in the hull of a slave ship. They had to be strong to endure slavery, prejudice, Jim Crow, racism, discrimination, and poverty. To God Be the Glory…through me they made it through.

Today I have what my grandmother called "Perfect Peace". "The kind of peace that goes beyond all understanding". I've never been happier with myself, for myself, and by myself. It's a wonderful place to be, a FANTASTIC time in my life to just be me.

As I Am Reminded…

A Gracious Woman

The most memorable week of my life, no doubt out of the more than 2,900 weeks I've been blessed to be on earth has to be Friday, March 27, 2014 thru Friday, April 4, 2014.

Would you believe that on Saturday, March 28, 2014 the transmission in my 15-year-old van died? Monday, April 30, 2014, my sweet little dog Wesley died of cancer. Then, on Friday, April 4, 2014 my wonderful mother, Mrs. Elizabeth Angloria deMontagnac made her transition to be with the lord.

OMG, I prayed for the strength of my grandmother, my great grandmother, my great great, great grandmother, and my great great great great grandmother's sprits to surround me. I asked to be empowered with the courage I needed to get through this trio of unexpected events.

Again, I took a deep breath…and kept it moving. Mother's home going service was as amazing as she was. Her service was at her home church in Baltimore, Maryland; Falls Road AME. Rev. Raymond F. Edmonds, Jr., preached a mighty, mighty sermon about the "Gracious Women". He gave a wonderful testament to my mother, who was always the epitome of femininity, grace, and who's true desire is to be a women of service in the Kingdom of God; always willing to serve.

A bright, warm sunny day filled with love, friends, family, and a special appearance by my dear friend Steve.

121

When I spoke to Steve the night before Moms funeral, he was looking for a flight out of Los Angeles. He and his handler Francis, caught the red eye into Washington Dulles International Airport, got into a limo and rode an hour or more to Baltimore. He tried to check into his hotel, at 8:00 a.m., his room wasn't ready.

Steve and Francis changed their clothes in the locker room of the hotel gym. They got back into the limo and drove thirty-five more minutes to the church.

Steve arrived at the church at the perfect time. I had already given remarks, my Nephew Damion who is the first grandson, and my niece Nikiya who is the first granddaughter, told some amazing stories about their Nana. My daughter Nadera recited a poem she had written about my mother called, 100 Day's with Honey Bunny. Nadera made everyone laugh, smile, and shared the joy of the fond memories she had of living with her grandmother for one hundred days.

My grandmother's pastor was sitting in the pulpit; he motioned to me that Steve had just walked in the sanctuary. While I was making my remarks, I explained to the crowed that we will be having a wonderful surprise very soon, so just be patient.

I walked down the aisle to meet him and Francis. Completely overjoyed I took his hand and lead him to the front pew. He whispered in my ear, "Has anyone done the Lord's Prayer?" I said "no". Steve asked me to tell the pianist to play it in F sharp. Francis escorted Steve to the microphone; he pulled his harmonica out of his jacket pocket and started to play. After he finished playing The Lord's Prayer he began to sing it. Oh my Jesus, all our hearts were so full of comfort, peace, happiness, and love as we listened to him perform for mother. As always, Steve came that day to give honor to my mother, and to show his unyielding kindness for all whose life he touches.

To see the way people respond to him is sometimes quite hilarious. As we were leaving the church, people were trying to get pictures with him, asking for autographs. The real kicker was when the gentleman who was pushing my mom's casket into the hearse stopped, pulled out his flip phone, took a photo of Steve and me. He then put his phone back into his pocket; and without missing a beat, pushed mom's casket into the hearse. You truly see the best and worst of people at funerals.

Steve spent the entire day with us, were we standing in the mausoleum, and he said to me that remembered the sounds the workers were making as they were preparing the casket to be placed in the wall of the mausoleum, it reminded him of his mother Lula's internment process sounds he said he would never forget.

When we returned to the church for the repass, I suggested that his driver take him a vegan restaurant near downtown, because all the food prepared for us at the repass contained some sort of meat. Steve has been on a vegan diet for almost two years now; and he says that he's seeing...Great results. (He is always making jokes about his blindness. Lol.)

Steve took Nadera with him to eat. While at the restaurant he greatly enjoyed a vegan meal, and stopped into a few shops on the same street to meet the locals and take photos. Steve's next stop was to visit a friend with a guitar store in a mall not far from the restaurant. Someone tweeted that Stevie Wonder is in the mall. Nadera said people came swarming towards him like bees racing to the hive. In fact, the local news outlets ran a story about Steve being in town for almost four days after mom's funeral.

To experience the transition of a loved one, especially a mother like mine. Her legacy will live in my heart forever, and I will continue to listen to her words of wisdom as she speaks to me in my dreams. Ms. Elizabeth has left me a plethora of great memories of her being an awesome, incredible, loving, caring, kind, funny, gracious, sweet, elegant, supportive, encouraging, and a godly woman.

Coping with death and other hardships of the heart are never easy. John 14:26-28 says, "But the Comforter, which is the Holy Ghost, whom the Father will send in my name, he shall teach you all things, and bring all things to your remembrance, whatsoever I have said unto you. Peace I leave with you, my peace I give unto you: not as the world giveth, give I unto you. Let not your heart be troubled, neither let it be afraid. Ye have heard how I said unto you, I go away, and come again unto you. If ye loved me, ye would rejoice, because I said, I go unto the Father: for my Father is greater than I. And now I have told you before it come to pass, that, when it is come to pass, ye might believe." (John 14:26-29 KJVA)

Before my mom transitioned, I was having some issues with her trying to maintain her independence. Her equilibrium was off, and she was using oxygen to help with her breathing. Mom started losing her balance, and falling as she tried to attempt to do the normal things she was accustomed to doing. I threatened to send her to Maryland where she has two brothers, Arnold, and Douglas, one sister, Geraldine (who transitioned forty-five days after mom) two daughters, Gale and Debbie, and a host of grandchildren, and great grandchildren.

One day I was trying to explain to her why it would be better for her in Maryland. My mom looked at me and said, "Ten of them don't equal one of you." We never had that discussion ever again.

A few days later, I was talking to my friend, Marvin, about what my mother had told me. He then said, "She's getting the royal treatment; why would she want to leave?" The night before my mother's funeral I wrote this for her.

Debbie, Gale, Mom, Junior & Little Stevie

The Hotel Royal

There's a place I know where only special people are invited to go. The Hotel Royal, it's not a very big place; it doesn't have Italian crystal chandlers, mosaic tiles on the floors, or priceless works of art by Picasso on the walls. No not any of those things.

The Hotel Royal is a spiritual dwelling that doesn't take American Express or Visa, but it's still priceless. A complete breakfast, with prayer, scripture, and a side of mediation, served up daily with all the other fixings like fruit, eggs, and turkey beacon. Can't forget the Cheerios with milk chilled to perfection which is served everyday on an old wooden TV tray. Piping hot coffee filled with octane made your way with French vanilla creamer, and one pack of Splenda. Oh want a wonderful place to spend your final days.

The Hotel Royal's superior staff is trained by the Big Fella upstairs, whose only request is to be of service, always showing how much you really care.

In the early part of the afternoon after a quick nap, it's time for a relaxing massage to relieve the aching pain that's nesting in your lower back. Oh what a refreshing moment of the day now that the pain has gone away.

Fresh flowers delivered to your room every week, a daily basket filled with all your favorite goodies and treats. A barrage of westerns for your viewing pleasure, from John Wayne, to Clint Eastwood, even Roy Rodgers and Trigger too. The Hotel Royal will always make your day.

When the sun sets on another perfect day, at the Hotel Royal you pick up another Harlequin Romance Novel and let Calgone take you away.
While finishing your last spoon full of your favorite carrot soufflé, realizing that the Hotel Royal has helped your pain go away.

The Big Fella gets your message that you're ready to leave and sends the angel valet to set you free. The angel valet orders the Rolls Royce Phantom to come pick you up. With twinkling lights that look like stars in the ceiling, the ride to heaven, what an amazing feeling.

Like heaven on earth, what an amazing space, the hotel Royal is filled with Gods love, patience, grace and un-yielding faith.

An anointed place for my mom Elizabeth Angloria deMontagnac to spend her final days…I call my home "The Hotel Royal".

Mrs. Elizabeth Angloria deMontagnac

July 2, 1935 – April 4, 2014

Queens of Courage

WOMEN WHO LOST THE BATTLE TO
BREAST CANCER BUT PUT UP AN
AWESOME FIGHT!!!!

Ernestine Fike	Mamie Brisco
Ercell Datcher	Ora Jordan
Vernetta Morgan	Minnie Riperton
Carla Allen	Gina Cook
Gloria Williamson	Mae McCray
Sophia Echols	Sophia Echols
Kim P. Harbison	Norma Cantrell
Shaunta D. Flowers	Kathy Haskins
Rose Mary Jones	Catrina Matthews
Helen Lucas	Dorothy Saleem
Maureen Vaughan	Majorie Roberts
Merlene Lockridge	Janet Walker
Charity Boatman	Marlyn Boatman
Annette Tomlinson	Lois Murray

RESOURCE GUIDE

GENERAL RESOURCES

AMC Cancer Research Center's Cancer Information Line
1-800-525-3777
www.amc.org

AMERICAN CANCER SOCIETY (ACS)
1-800-ACS-2345 (1-800-227-2345)
www.cancer.org

ASSOCIATION OF CANCER ONLINE RESOURCES
1-212-226-5525
www.acor.org

BREASTCANCER.NET
www.breastcancer.net

BREASTCANCER.ORG
www.breastcancer.org

CANCERINDEX.ORG
www.cancerindex.org

CANCERLINKS.ORG
www.cancerlinks.org

CHEMOCARE.COM
www.chemocare.com

NATIONAL CANCER INSTITUTE (NCI)
1-800-4-CANCER (1-800-422-6237)
www.cancer.gov

ADVOCACY GROUPS / ORGANIZATIONS

AVON BREAST CRUSADE
www.avoncrusade.com

NATIONAL BREAST CANCER COALITION
1-202-296-7477
www.natlbccc.org

NATIONAL COALITION FOR CANCER SURVIVORSHIP
1-877-622-7937
www.canceradvocacy.org

PATIENT ADVOCATE FOUNDATION
1-800-532-5274
www.patientadvocate.org

SUSAN G. KOMEN FOR THE CURE
1-877-GO-KOMEN (1-877-465-6636)
www.komen.org

BREAST RECONSTRUCTION

AMERICAN CANCER SOCIETY
www.cancer.org

BREAST CANCER.ORG
www.breastcancer.org

BREAST IMPLANTS
1-888-463-6332
www.fda.gov

CENTER FOR MICROSURGICAL BREAST RECONSTRUCTION
www.diepflap.com

MEDLINE PLUS
www.nlm.nih.gov

COMPLIMENTARY AND ALTERNATIVE MEDICINE

GLYCEMIC INDEX
www.southbeach-diet-plan.com

OFFICE OF DIETARY SUPPLEMENTS (ODS) NIH
www.ods.od.nih.gov

NATIONAL COUNCIL AGAINST HEALTH FRAUD
www.ncahf.org

U.S. FOOD AND DRUG ADMINISTRATION (FDA)
www.fda.gov/Food/default.htm

CANCER TREATMENTS CLINICAL ASPECTS

Cancer.gov: Breast Cancer Clinical Trials
www.cancer.gov/clinicaltrials

Inflammatory Breast Cancer (IBC) Research Foundation
www.ibcresearch.org

National Cancer Institute
www.cancer.gov

National Comprehensive Cancer Network
Breast Cancer Treatment Guidelines for Patients
www.nccn.org

CHILDREN AND FAMILIES

Caring Bridge
www.caringbridge.org

Kids Konnected
1-800-899-2866
www.kidskonnected.org

EMPLOYMENT CONCERNS

American Cancer Society – Americans with Disabilities Act
www.cancer.org

Family and Medical Leave Act
1-866-4-US-WAGE (1-866-487-9243)

National Coalition for Cancer Survivorship
(NCCS) Employment
www.canceradvocacy.org

The US Equal Opportunity Commission
www.eeoc.gov

HAIR CARE AND MAKE-UP

Look Good…Feel Better
1-800-395-LOOK (5665)

INSURANCE AND FINANCES

Cancer.Net
www.cancer.net/patient/Library/Financial+Resources

Georgetown University Health Policy Institute
www.healthisuranceinfo.net

National Coalition for Cancer Survivorship (NCCS) Insurance
www.canceradvocacy.org

PREGNANCY AND BREAST CANCER

BreastCancer.org
www.breastcancer.org

Fertile Hope
www.fertilehope.org

Hope for Two: Pregnant with Cancer Network
1-800-743-4471
www.pregnantwithcancer.org

LYMPHDEMA

National Lymphedema Network
1-800-541-3259
www.lymphnet.org

PROSTHESIS

ReForma
http://myreforma.com

Softee
1-866-594-8585
www.softeeusa.com

SEXUALITY

International Academy of Compounding Pharmacies
1-800-927-4227
www.iacprx.org

Pure Romance
1-866-ROMANCE
www.pureromance.com

SUPPORT GROUPS / ORGANIZATIONS

African-American Breast Cancer Alliance (AABCA)
1-800-ACS-2345
www.geocities.com/aabcainc

Breast Cancer Network of Strength
1-800-221-2141 (24-hour hotline – English)
1-800-986-9505 (24-hour hotline – Spanish)
www.networkofstrength.org

Sisters Network Inc. (African-American Women)
1-866-781-1808
www.sistersnetworkinc.org

The Wellness Community
1-202-659-9709
www.thewellnesscommunity.org

Yes, I Can Action Now
www.yesicannow.org

The Young Survival Coalition (Young Women)
1-877-972-1011

SURGERY

Breast Cancer Network of Strength
1-800-221-2141 (24-hour hotline – English)
1-800-986-9505 (24-hour hotline – Spanish)
www.networkofstrength.org

Caring Connections
www.caringinfo.org/stateaddownload

Epilogue:
"Purpose in My Pain"

By Rev. Dr. William Holmes Robinson

God has a purpose behind every problem He is allowing you and me to go through - difficult circumstances and hardships - so we can find a sense of His purpose in our lives. God will use circumstances sometimes to develop our character. None of us is immune to pain or insulated from suffering. Life is a series of problems. As you resolve one, another one is waiting to take its place. Jesus warned us in John 16:33, "In the world you would have tribulations: but be of good cheer; I have overcome the world." James said it this way in James 1:2, "My brethren, count it all joy when you fall into various trials." Even Job 14:1 says, "Man that is born of a woman is of few days, and full of trouble."

Sometimes, being in the will of God and being in His purpose mean going through some difficult times. We think how we can be in the will of God when He allows us to have pain. Because we are feeling pain, it is not necessarily bad.

The good news is we can feel. And if we can feel, we can move ourselves from harm's way.

A doctor may cause pain, but after he cuts us, the healing begins. And I've discovered pain is just what we need to develop our character. We go through and not stay in situations that cause us pain. God uses problems to develop our character. Our most intimate days of worship are during our darkest days. When our hearts are broken, our pride is stripped away and we are feeling low, God can work with us.

And I really want to reassure someone reading this that is going through trouble in your life right now that your trouble won't last long. I wish I could tell somebody today that if you just take an aspirin for your troubles, in the morning everything will be all right. I wish I could tell you that your marriage is going to be saved in about three hours, but I can't tell you that your trouble won't last long. But I can tell you, however, that your trouble won't last always. The songwriter said, "I'm so glad that trouble doesn't last always." The psalmist said it this way, "Weeping may endure for a night, but joy cometh in the morning."

Through it all, I have learned to lean on God, to put my trust in the Master's hand. He has brought me out of darkness in to the light of day. I know my trials have come to make me strong. God has brought me a mighty long way. And, truly, there is purpose in my pain.

My Name Is Stevie Flowers and I'm a Survivor

Made in the
USA
Columbia, SC